Literacy as Involvement

Literacy as Involvement:

The Acts of Writers, Readers, and Texts

Deborah Brandt

Southern Illinois University Press

Carbondale and Edwardsville

14 13 12 11   4 3 2 1

Library of Congress Cataloging-in-Publication Data
Brandt, Deborah, 1951–
        Literacy as involvement : the acts of writers, readers, and texts / Deborah
        Brandt. — Pbk. ed.
            p. cm.
        Includes bibliographical references and index.
    ISBN-13: 978-0-8093-3038-6 (pbk. : alk. paper)
    ISBN-10: 0-8093-3038-5 (pbk. : alk. paper)
    ISBN-13: 978-0-8093-8785-4 (ebook)
    ISBN-10: 0-8093-8785-9 (ebook)
    1. Written communication. 2. Literacy. 3. Discourse analysis. I. Title.
    P211.B695 2011
    302.2'244—dc22   2010047586

For my two involvements:
Steve and Mike Wajda

Contents

Acknowledgments

The idea for writing a book about the acts of writing and reading and what they have to say about the nature of literacy first flickered into my consciousness in 1982 as I sat in a delicatessen in downtown Bloomington, Indiana. I was fortunate to be studying at the time at Indiana University with Marilyn Sternglass in writing theory and Jerome Harste in reading theory. Their seminars, freewheeling, disputatious, insistently interdisciplinary, brought issues of literacy to me in urgent and exciting ways. Much has changed since 1982, but the intellectual food that Marilyn and Jerry served up still sustains me. So my foremost thanks are to them. I also must thank another ex-Indiana mentor, David Bleich, who listened to me complaining one day that too much that was written about literacy was bogged down in arguments over values. "How can you write about literacy," Bleich demanded, "without writing about values?" It took me several years—and several false starts on this work—to understand what he meant.

I wish to thank several other people who read various drafts and portions of this book and to absolve them of any responsibility for lingering misjudgments or errors. They are Eugene Kintgen, Martin Nystrand, Charles Read, and, especially, Nick Doane for particularly insightful responses. I also want to thank the anonymous reviewers for Southern Illinois University Press for helpful criticisms that I hope and believe have made this a better book. Thanks to Mike Rose and Steve Witte for their kind support at a critical time. Several colleagues and friends have talked over the project with me, even when they probably did not want to. I thank Carol Pasternack, Brad Hughes, Melanie Schneider, Tom Fox, Eli Goldblatt, and my dear friends Beth Kalikoff and Randall Knoper, who, I think, were with me in the delicatessen and have stayed close across the miles and years. Randolph Brandt, a writer I admire very much, offered astute advice from time to time. Kenney Withers, director of Southern Illinois University Press, has overseen this project with care, sensitivity, and efficiency. I thank him for his patience and support. Thanks also to Stephen W. Smith for insightful copyediting. Deanna Briley and Julie Palmer cheerfully spun versions of the manuscript out of their printers and generally kept order in the chaos. I also thank the American Council of Learned Societies and the University of Wisconsin Graduate School for providing research fellowships in the fall of 1986 that allowed me to begin work on the book. A final, inadequate word of thanks to Steve Wajda for his capacious and forbearing love.

Literacy as Involvement

Introduction

To ask "What is literacy?" is to ask, most of all, how literacy is to be understood. For some, literacy is a technology; for others, a cognitive consequence; for still others, a set of cultural relationships; yet for others, a part of the highest human impulse to think and rethink experience in place. Literacy is a complex phenomenon, making problems of perspective and definition inevitable. Literacy is also something of real value, making struggle around it unlikely to end.

The basic questions of this study have to do with how literacy is to be understood. The study addresses, and attempts to resolve, a certain paradox in current understandings of literacy, a paradox whose patterns run through my own field of composition studies, as well as through research on emergent (preschool) literacy and the difficult issues of literacy failures in school. The paradox goes this way: On the one hand, it is written language that makes us distinctly creatures of culture. Other animals communicate; only humans read and write. Those things that contribute most to the collective sense, such as history or law, could come only with the invention of writing. And in their communicative functions, of course, reading and writing serve to close up the spaces between people, to draw them together across the impediments of time and space. Functionally speaking, literacy is the most social of all imaginable practices—hypersocial, actually, because it epitomizes the role of culture in human exchange and condenses into the channels of reading and writing some of the most crucial of our joint enterprises. To read or write is to trade heartily—inescapably—on commonality and collectivity. That is why being illiterate in a literate culture is so isolating. To be illiterate is to be without important means to trade with others.

Yet there is another current that says to be literate one must be able to pull away from the demanding solidarity with the social world, to put deliberate space and time *between* oneself and others. "The book, like the door," writes David Riesman, "is an encouragement to isolation" (112). Readers, according to Myron Tuman, "require the psychological motivation to separate themselves from what they share with others" (31). In a familiar cultural motif, the third-world villager or working-class scholarship student who goes off to school and becomes literate is forever estranged from home, ruined, in a sense, by a new and irreconcilable way of being in the world. From this perspective the hypersociability of literacy appears as abstractness. Written language removes social life to a symbolic realm to be contemplated or manipulated mentally and privately. To engage in reading or writing is to be willing and able to follow written language into that realm. Our human contact, laundered through the disembodied conventions of language-on-its-own, can only be abstractly rendered and perceived. Literacy alienates; it requires an attitude of alienation, a surrender of *common* sense in order to work. In these two versions of literacy, then, the illiterate and the committed literate wind up together—on the outside.

This social/antisocial tension flashes in many current issues in composition studies: To what extent is social cognition significant in writing ability? How valid are conversation-based approaches to writing development? Is the writer's audience really a fiction? This tension is perhaps most prominent in issues of school literacy success and failure. Children who do well in school tend to live lives outside of school that are richly dependent on literacy. They belong to households where reading and writing connect members to the world and to each other in tangible and often pleasurable ways. In other words, they experience literacy as connection and collectivity. Yet the cause of their success in school, according to researchers like David R. Olson and Catherine Snow, is a growing attitude of detachment, an ability to separate language from people. Thus, paradoxically, literacy seems to involve an intense contextualization of decontextualization, an intense socialization into antisocial ways with language. This same analysis, in reverse, is used to explain school literacy failures. Children from social groups that use language primarily to maintain social solidarity and context-resonant meaning will be at risk as readers and writers for their language orientation is deemed antiliterate.

Thus, the view that literacy requires "shutting the door" on everyday social experience has powerfully influenced the way that literacy problems have come to be labeled and the way that certain language habits have been deemed favorable or unfavorable to literacy development. But what are the assumptions that underlie this antisocial characterization? And does it indeed describe the social and cognitive orientations that reading and writing demand?

My aim is to look hard at the foundations of this antisocial view of literacy in order to offer a reformulation of the nature of literate language and the social processes that spawn it. Antisocial characterizations arise from what could be called a "strong-text" account of literacy and literate language, which posits a radical rupture between the person-to-person sense-making of oral discourse and the very different interpretive demands posed by written language. Strong-text characterizations derive from a view of literate language as decontextualized (that is "de-situated") and self-referential. Inscribed language is said to rise clear of an embeddedness in an immediate time, place, and voice, thereby objectifying thought and language and heightening consciousness of both in a way that permits the reorganization of both. Freed from what Paul Ricoeur calls a "grounding of reference in the dialogical situation" (34), written language supposedly sheds the deictic quality of oral language and becomes genuinely self-referential. The context for literate discourse is no longer the ordinary social world but a world of pure words (and by extension the world of pure texts), worlds no longer beholden to the ordinary world or to social relationships within that world.

Sometimes the "great escape" of writing is expressed as a freeing of language from a necessary syncopation with pragmatic action. Literate language is seen as the medium for private contemplation and reflection, in which formal language overwhelms consciousness and becomes an independent locus of meaning. In this view, literate language does not so much convey or share a message as it objectifies it. And, as it does, objectification becomes part of the message. This self-referentiality and strong internal structuring of literate language is said to be reflected in the nature of typical expository prose, which is usually described as detached, explicit, and message-dense, sparse in the interpersonal devices that are rife in conversation. According to many literacy theorists, this lifting out and distancing of *form*al language is what permits the development of formal reasoning, which Valerie Walkerdine defines as a conscious reflection on "the internal relations of statements themselves" (138) and which, as Jack Goody contends, enables the capacity for syllogistic reasoning.[1] Myron Tuman sees the decontextualized nature of literate language and the decontextualized interpretive habits it inspires to be the source of literacy's power. Written language allows meaning to be resymbolized beyond the constraints of what he calls "ordinary social experience" (17), allowing us to imagine alternate, possible, and resistant worlds.

In strong-text characterizations, literacy is a branch of language development that is distinct from—even, in a sense, antagonistic to—oral language development. Of course, many strong-text proponents, including Goody, Walter J. Ong, and David R. Olson, recognize the "interminglings" and "interfaces" of the oral and the literate (or what Deborah Tannen on occasion has called the oral-like and the literate-like to point up that spoken discourse can readily take on literate form and function just as written texts can resemble the forms and functions of talk).[2] Nevertheless, learning to read and write is thought to require a new way with language, a new set of interpretive rules and social realignments in which meaning is made out of language-on-its-own, without direct appeal to intersubjective orientation or to a local context of pragmatic action. To stay wedded to the latter, oral-like methods of interpretation is, in the strong-text analysis, to risk literacy failure.

This study offers a different interpretation of written texts and the demands of literate orientation. It does so by returning to the key foundations in strong-text formulations: context and reference. I will argue that the interpretive dynamic among context, reference, and meaning fundamentally does not change in the move from the oral to the literate. Literate language does indeed derive its meaning from local contexts of practical action—namely the here-and-now, intersubjective actions of writing and reading. Writers and readers in action are deeply embedded in an immediate working context of aims, plans, trials, and constructions (which themselves are tied to circumstantial and cultural contexts of all sorts). The language that they write and read finds meaning only in relationship to this ongoing context—a context more of work than of words. Further, reference in literate language is also context-bound and essentially deictic, pointing not in at internal relations of a text but out to the developing here-and-now relationship of writer and reader at work. Texts talk incessantly about the acts of writing and reading in progress. No matter what their ostensible topic, written texts are primarily about the writing and reading of them. What they refer to is not an explicit message but the implicit process by which intersubjective understanding is getting accomplished. That is what you have to know in order to read and write.

This reformulation becomes clear from the perspective being opened up by recent research on writing and reading processes. Process research is still a relatively new area of inquiry and has been limited by what critics rightly see as a too narrow focus on isolated cognitive operations. Nevertheless, process-centered research, such as the think-aloud protocol research of Flower and Hayes at Carnegie-Mellon University, offers suggestive new glimpses into literacy-in-action, insights which should be accommodated in any definition of literacy or literacy development. At a most basic level, process studies situate literate language at the sites of composing and construing. Transcripts of the minute-by-minute thinking of writers and readers are a reminder of what hard work writing and reading are and how much the meaning of a text depends on the nature of the work being done. Whether based on human think-aloud reports or computer simulations, process descriptions of reading and writing resort to the language not of logic nor semantic networks but to the language of pragmatic action (goals, plans, scenarios, situations, etc.). From a process perspective, writing and reading activity appears to be instigated and guided by considerations that do not originate in contemplation of the "internal relations of statements themselves."

Process studies reveal a double reference in textual language. While text-centered analyses focus on explicit grammatical, syntactic, and semantic ties within a physically decontextualized text, protocol research particularly shows how the meaning of textual language is tied to what is going on in a writer's or reader's here-and-now working context. To make a text mean, writers and readers have to see what it is saying about what they are doing or ought to be doing, Texts are not merely outcomes of reading and writing processes; they are deeply about those processes. Thus, the first requirement for understanding texts is understanding that they refer to what people do with them. As a later chapter will explore in more depth, the ability to read and write with awareness of this double reference ("what a text is saying and what it is saying about what I am supposed to doing") distinguishes effective readers and writers from less effective ones.

What implications does a process view hold for characterizing literacy and literate development, particularly vis-à-vis prevailing, strong-text conceptions? In prevailing views, literacy is said to require subordinating intersubjective channels in order to focus primarily on message or content. The "what" of written discourse takes precedence over the "who." The key knowledge for literacy development, from strong-text perspectives, is knowing how language can work as a detached and self-referential system of meaning. This study argues that, on the contrary, literacy requires heightening awareness of how language works to sustain intersubjectivity, particularly the intersubjective work of reading and writing. This intersubjectivity is deeper and more particular than rhetorical considerations of audience and persona or even the general ability to recognize and anticipate the viewpoints of others (although these factors are clearly important in the development of literate ability).[3] Rather, it is a fundamental, enabling awareness of the mutual work that is under way around an unfolding text, a growing understanding of how language and work (text and context) constitute each other. Learning to read is learning that you are being written to, and learning to write is learning that your words are being read.

The highly metacommunicative nature of writing and reading suggests that the key knowledge for literate development is knowing about how people read and write, how they do the work of it. That knowledge is the crucial context that brings sense to written language. This explains why literacy learning requires not merely ample experience with print but ample access to other people who read and write and who will show you why and how they do it.

Such a reformulation of the basis of literate development calls into question prevailing characterizations of oral-literate relationships. First, as I mentioned, literacy learning poses the same basic interpretive puzzles as oral language learning, which as Michael Halliday has established, involves figuring out how language and occasion work to bring meaning to each other, how together they realize social reality (*Language as Social Semiotic*). This functional, pragmatic syncopation of language and context is what opens children to the world of talk, the world *as* talk (Halliday, *Learning How to Mean*). The same relationship pertains in confronting print. I do not mean to suggest here that there are no significant differences between oral and literate language and their uses—only that the differences do not arise from a change in the pragmatic relationship between context and language.

Further, literacy learning requires intensifying—not subordinating—reliance on social involvement as a basis of interpretation in reading and writing. It requires heightening understanding of how human beings create reality together. In oral exchanges, this joint reality-making is at once both more obvious (because speakers are physically together) and more hidden (because we tend to think of the oral context as already "there" and so are less conscious of the degree, even in talk, that language contributes to the forging of a shared world). In written language, these illusions are less tenable; the social foundations of reality (how we work together to bring reality into being) become more fully crystallized. Writing and reading are pure acts of human involvement.

Now one might argue that what I have just presented is but a slight and ultimately even trivial adjustment in the strong-text case, for I too link literacy with a heightened consciousness of language and the workings of language. But the difference I want to draw (and especially the ramifications of that difference) is far from trivial. Literacy is not a matter of learning to go it alone with language but learning to go it alone with each other. It is not a matter of learning how statements stick together but rather how people stick together through literate means.

The radically social foundations of the literate orientation compel a reanalysis of literacy failures in school. In the prevailing view, students fail to the extent to which they fail to treat language objectively and separately from people (including themselves), fail to appreciate the new (i.e., "unsocial," "unoral") stances that literacy demands. This study rejects such an explanation. Theories of literacy based on the need for "decontextualization" of thought and language often justify instructional practices that may mislead struggling students, deflecting them from the very sorts of clues they need to figure out reading and writing. More troubling, to characterize as antiliterate any language habits that value shared orientation and social solidarity is to foreclose on what in fact is the richest foundation of literacy. Learning to read requires learning to maintain—in fact, intensify—reliance on social context even under new and precarious circumstances. Literacy failures are not failures of separation but rather failures of involvement. They arise not from an overdependence on context but from the lack of access to a viable context for making sense of print.

Instead of viewing the oral as antagonistic to the literate, it is necessary to understand better how the oral sustains the literate. If the key knowledge for literacy development is finding out how people *do* reading and writing, then literacy is indeed dependent on oral transmissions, for this knowledge must be passed mouth-to-mouth, person-to-person. Literacy ceases to be an abstract, text-engined technology in tension with local practices and loyalties and instead appears as something that flourishes only in local forms, as part of "how we do things around here." It is by nature and necessity pluralistic and in flux. This conclusion has been reached from a cultural perspective from, among others, psychologists Sylvia Scribner and Michael Cole, historian Harvey Graff, and ethnographer Shirley Brice Heath. This study attempts to advance a similar conclusion from a look at particular acts of writers, readers, and texts.

An Overview of the Study

Chapter One examines the prevailing strong-text view of literacy, as articulated by Walter J. Ong, Jack Goody, David R. Olson, and others. The discussion centers upon common assumptions in their depictions of literate orientation and especially how they come to identify literacy with social detachment. In strong-text descriptions, literacy is said to be induced by the unique technological powers of written language, powers that force attention away from the world and onto the text. In this view, the requisites for literacy appear indistinguishable from the qualities of texts. To be literate one must be textlike: logical, literal, detached, and message-focused. The significant literate relationship is with the text. This model of literacy has been used, especially by Olson, to describe the language transition that school demands. To succeed at school, according to Olson, students must be able to transcend dependency on social context and make meaning out of the fixed, semantic resources of language-on-its-own.

Strong-text accounts of literacy are product-centered, defining literacy by working backward from the nature of finished texts. Chapter Two counters the claims of strong-text advocates by setting out a view of literacy based on the cognitive work that the processes of writing and reading require. From such a process orientation literacy appears as the ability *to keep writing or reading going*. It is the ability to manage an event, an event that does not very much resemble a text. We will look at the sorts of things people need to do in order to keep acts of reading and writing going, including the need to maintain involvement with what Ragnar Rommetveit calls the "temporarily shared social reality" that a text is realizing. The chapter looks closely at process-oriented research in writing, including the pioneering work of Linda Flower and John R. Hayes. Their research has contributed to a process-sensitivity in the teaching of writing and a deepened understanding of the complex concerns that go into making a text. But scant attention has been given to the significance of this research for reinterpreting literacy and literate processes. Several of their key findings are pertinent: the differences between expert and novice writers, the social significance of the changing dynamics of plans during composing, and what Flower and Hayes call "current meaning" in a writer's decision-making.

A process perspective on composing reveals two related points that must inform understandings of literacy. First, writing is not merely a matter of preparing a text for an eventual reader but also a matter of maintaining the conditions that keep writing itself going. The ability to manage the process, whether reading or writing, is the essence of literate orientation. Second, texts are not merely the goal of writing, the output, but the public means by which writers keep writing. Writers (like readers) have to know what an unfolding text means for things on their end—what a text is saying about what they need to be doing. Thus, becoming literate is not learning how to divorce language from action; rather, becoming literate is coming to understand the action that written language relates to. To learn to read and write one must figure out the metacommunicative meanings of written discourse—how flat marks on a flat page talk about the joint actions of a writer and a reader.

Seeing texts more fully in relationship to the processes that produce them allows for a more socially sensitive interpretation of their basic features. The familiar elements of so-called message-focused, autonomous texts take on a different meaning when viewed as they are coming over the horizon, so to speak, for writers in the act of composing and readers in the act of comprehending. Chapter Three traces the abundant allusions to the acts of writing and reading in typical "decontextualized"discourse. Even the most literal-seeming textual statements carry "undertalk" that speaks of a developing involvement between writer and reader-in-the-act. The chapter treats several texts to demonstrate how they overtly and covertly refer to the unfolding acts of writing and reading and to the general sense of "what is going on here." Discussion centers on several key text features, including cohesion, labeling, and lexical variety, as they function as part of the involvement-focus of written discourse. These features are generally considered the message-focused hallmarks of autonomous exposition, but from a social perspective they appear to sustain much of the metacommunicative undertalk by which writing and reading are managed. The aim is to show how the familiar apparatus of written texts, rather than serving to separate an explicit message from an implicit context, is very explicit about that implicit context.

Chapter Four treats writer-reader involvement as it relates to rhetorical issues of discourse. Several texts are analyzed at length to show how a writer's developing intimacy with a reader becomes the grounds for rhetorical activity. More aspects of textual undertalk are traced to show how readers, in accomplishing the intersubjective grounds necessary for understanding a text, gain perspective on its rhetorical dimension.

Finally, Chapter Five returns to the larger issues of literacy and involvement to reassess some of the issues associated with school literacy and especially to question the theory that students need to learn how to decontextualize language as a first and crucial step. Instead, the chapter argues that the key to becoming literate is finding out how other people read and write and how print relates to what people do when they read and write. The chapter calls for conceptions of literacy that are more process-centered, more realistic, and ultimately less disenfranchising.

Literacy vs. the Ability to Read and Write

It is common in discussions of literacy to try to extend its definition beyond the "mere ability" to read and write. Myron Tuman, in *A Preface to Literacy,* for instance, rejects what he calls the "unproblematic model" of literacy that equates it with simple skills of decoding or encoding written language—a model he finds dominating the schools and literacy testing (9–15). One can read and write, he says, and still fail to engage in metaphorical meaning-making, which, in his estimation, is the genuine literate enterprise. Robert Pattison in *On Literacy* makes the intriguing argument that a person in a sense already has to be literate in order to read and write because, in his view, literacy is a broad "consciousness of the problems posed by language" (vi), a consciousness that enables and informs particular acts of reading or writing. Political critiques frequently fault narrow, technical "decoding" definitions of literacy for trying to conceal ideological interests in the neutral language of "skills" or "abilities" and for failing to consider social injustices that lie behind— even insure—failures in reading and writing.[4] What Tuman, Pattison, and others hold in common is a belief that literacy is something more than a mundane language skill.

I am sympathetic to these criticisms and circumspect about the social and political complexities surrounding literacy and any assertions about it (including my own). Yet this study rather adamantly focuses on the "mere ability" to read and write texts, particularly expository ones. Such a focus reflects my practical concern that many Americans (twenty-five million adult Americans, at minimum, by Jonathan Kozol's estimates) do not own the mere ability to read, despite years of schooling, and my concern that this failure has largely to do with the ineffective ways reading is presented in school. Further, I want to argue that the mere ability to read and write is far from simple and unproblematic. The ability to see sense in written language and to do something with it requires terrific coordination of language, knowledge, and social aware-ness. The trouble is not in treating literacy merely as decoding or encoding print but in underestimating how much is actually involved in those processes.

On Literacy and Composition Studies

Before moving on, one more related word is in order about the inspiration for this study. For the last few years, the field of composition has been struggling to resolve a split between social and cognitive views of writing. The perspectives have been glaringly different and difficult to bridge. Socially oriented research has illuminated the degree to which literacy is embedded in and shaped by cultural, political, and rhetorical processes. But these studies usually focus on big pictures—neighborhoods, classrooms, whole disciplines, or large chunks of historical time—with little consideration of how these big-picture constituencies come into play during individual acts of writing. On the other hand, the little pictures, such as the oral protocol studies of Flower and Hayes, describe writers caught up in the mental machinations of producing texts, working through the sweaty problems of setting goals, accessing knowledge, drafting, and revising, with very little reference to big-picture matters.

Both social and cognitive perspectives ask the same question: How do people write? But the "how" is interpreted differently. From the social perspective, the how pertains to ideological and cultural conditions that constitute and enable literacy as a social practice. It is a collective how. From the cognitive perspective, the how is interpreted in terms of the minute-by-minute work of individuals writing. While the social perspective takes for granted a certain technical ability to produce texts, it leaves the how of that ability unexamined. The cognitivists, in an attempt to map the dynamics of this technical ability, defer its connections to wider horizons. Each "side" tends to underproblematize the other perspective. Consequently, neither has developed much vocabulary with which to bridge the gap.

This gap is most pronounced in the way that the authored text is treated in the two orientations. Big-picture perspectives, if they deal with individual texts at all, absorb them into larger social and rhetorical categories. The integrity of an individual text is subordinated to the forces of which it becomes an emblem. On the cognitive side, the text has had an ambivalent status, partly because of the conscious movement away from product toward process. Additionally, texts in cognitive studies are treated as solutions, as the-end-of-the-line resolution of problems that are posed during composing. Texts appear as records of problems solved (more or less), rather than as documents that are themselves gaining problematic public life in social arenas.

If social and cognitive perspectives hope to come together, the text is the territory on which detente must begin. What are needed are ways to talk about texts as they relate to the processes of composing but also as those processes constitute public acts in social contexts. This study, although primarily focused on the border of cognition and text, offers one move in that effort.

Chapter One

Strong Text: Opacity, Autonomy, and Anonymity

"Literacy," according to William Frawley, "is equivalent to textuality" (33). What he means is that literacy is culturally dependent on the invention and continued existence of the technology of text. Literacy is the heat generated by the fire of textuality. Frawley also means that literacy lies in one's relationship with texts. Literacy, he says, is "the ability of individuals to deal with texts" (37).

This definition captures the essence of what can be called a "strong-text" explanation of literacy, an explanation that has been quite influential in shaping contemporary conceptions of literacy development and the causes of literacy failure. Strong text perspectives accord an extremely activist role to written language in precipitating and shaping literate orientation, both social and cognitive. In this view, people become literate by coming to terms with the unique demands of alphabetic writing, a technology that forces radical interpretive shifts away from oral discourse habits. Literacy, from this perspective, is said to entail a suppression of ordinary social involvement as the basis of interpretation and a reinvestment in the logical, literal, message-focused conventions of language-on-its-own.

This chapter traces the origins of strong-text assumptions, as they grow out of oral-literate contrasts generally and are represented in the work of a number of leading literacy theorists, including Jack Goody, Walter J. Ong, Deborah Tannen, and David R. Olson. My aim is to show how their characterizations of literacy are shaped with reference to written products, rather than to the acts (and actors) of writing and reading. As the major assumptions of strong-text theories are examined, it will become clear that they define the nature of literacy by working backward from the nature of texts. Most strong-text accounts give little consideration to the processes of writing and reading, to questions of how people actually accomplish literate acts in daily life.

When the focus moves from product to process, as it will in subsequent chapters, a much different picture of literacy emerges. From a process perspective, literacy does not take its nature from texts. Rather, texts take their natures from the ways that they are serving the acts of writing and reading. Further, from a process perspective, social involvement appears as a fundamental basis of orientation during the tenuous enterprises of writing and reading, making literacy not the narrow ability to deal with texts but the broad ability to deal with other people as a writer or a reader.

The discussion begins with a brief overview of oral-literate contrasts, since they are the point of departure for strong-text perspectives. Written texts appear "strong" to the extent to which they are contrasted with evanescent speech. They also gather strength to the extent to which they are seen to compensate for (and transform) the loss of oral opportunities.

Orality and Literacy

As an approach to language, oral-literate contrasts run deeply through anthropology, linguistics, psychology, and education. Anthropologists find the oral-literate framework useful in accounting for different social and economic arrangements in nonliterate and literate societies and for tracing the changes that occur in oral societies when they adopt and disseminate written language. Linguists attempt to characterize the structure of written discourse in terms of its similarities to and differences from the structure of spoken discourse. Some psychologists have attempted to gauge the cognitive impact that comes with the transition to print. And in education the framework has been used to articulate the transitions youngsters must make in moving from the primarily oral discourse of home to the discursive, scholastic discourse of the school.[1] Even popular debates about the "literacy crisis" rely on oral-literate dichotomies by pitting print against television and other forms of orally based media. Most recently scholars have acknowledged that orality and literacy are best understood as a continuum rather than a dichotomy and have advocated more sensitivity to the ways that the oral and the literate interpenetrate in everyday language use. Nevertheless orality and literacy tend to be treated in terms of their relationship to one another.

The chart below demonstrates how orality, speaking, and spoken discourse are typically contrasted with literacy, writing, and written discourse. They can be grouped according to three main concerns. The first, linguistic, has to do with how oral and written discourse are produced and structured, as well as the functions that they typically serve. Here the different circumstances of production, spontaneous dialogue versus planned monologue, account for significant surface differences in the two sorts of discourse. Speech stays close to the immediate surroundings and the immediate participants. Writing grows self-referential and message-focused as the burden of meaning falls more concentratedly on the words.

The second category, cognitive, has to do with the habits of mind that are typically associated with oral and literate approaches. The technology of writing is seen to open up new cognitive horizons, allowing extended thought to be externalized, preserved, and transformed. Oral thinking likewise reflects the circumstances of its production. Produced in the here and the now and the between us, oral discourse conserves thought primarily through mnemonic organization of language.

The third category, social/interpretive, reflects aspects of the other two categories. It has to do with the different attitudes and methods of interpretation that are called upon in oral and written discourse. The ways that speech and writing are produced influence the ways that meaning is produced in the two modes. Interpretation of speech stays close to the moment and the participants. Meaning is pragmatic, aimed at getting the immediate job done. Literate interpretation is more deliberate, reflective, and private, tied to the demands of formal language and not the demands of the pressing-in world. Social/interpretive treatments of orality and literacy also note that speech is natural, a universal and spontaneous outgrowth of one's membership in an immediate social group, while literacy is transmitted primarily through formal learning. That is, written language is not only produced under different circumstances from speech but must be learned under different circumstances, a difference which itself influences the outcome of meaning.

To explore a bit further the particulars of these oral-literate relationships, it will help to review briefly the ideas of several leading literacy theorists, all of whom, to one degree or another, attribute literacy to the "take off" of textuality.

Jack Goody and literate social structuring. As a social anthropologist primarily of the ancient Near East and modern Africa, Jack Goody attempts to account for the impact that writing has on cultural development and on the ways that literate people come to view themselves and each other under the new conditions that writing makes possible. At the heart of Goody's anthropological work is the recognition that communicative systems shape culture as much as religious or economic systems and that forms of society can be understood as forms of communication. He would agree with Raymond Williams who writes that "men and societies are not confined to relationships of power, property, and

Oral-Literate Contrast

	Oral	Literate
Linguistic	spontaneous	planned
	exophoric (refers outward)	endophoric (refers inward)
	lexically implicit	lexically explicit
	fragmented	integrated
	involvement-focused	message-focused
	(metacommunicative)	(propositional)
Cognitive	sensorimotor/perceptual	conceptual
	present tense	future/possible
	associative	objective
	formulaic, synthetic	analytical
	conformist	skeptical
Social/Interpretive	learned spontaneously	taught formally
	context-dependent	detached/distanced
	(situated)	(isolated)
	interactive	impersonal
	action based (communal)	reflection based (individual thought)
	interpreted in terms of speaker	interpreted in terms of what is on the page
	casual meaning	literal meaning
	"conversations are events not things"	"texts are things not events"

production. Their relationships in describing, learning, persuading, and exchanging experiences are . . . equally fundamental" (18). Writing, according to Goody, is intrinsic to our notions of modern social organizations. With writing came the capacity to separate from the undifferentiated collectivity of oral culture such distinct entities as formal religion, commerce, government, and law (*Logic of Writing*). Writing brings to the surface tacit rules and ideologies, allowing them to become more consciously formulated, codified, and bounded. Writing enhances religion, for instance, because it gives people an easier way to see the idea of religion and to conceive of religion, law, or civil administration as an institution with distinct discourses and distinguishable interests. In Goody's view, the material inscription of writing throws separateness into high material relief, enabling the fragmented, bureaucratic, hierarchical arrangements of modern (literate) societies. Knowledge in general also undergoes transformation as writing removes dialectic from dialogue, from the context, that is, of face-to-face encounters. Writing enables a new dialectic not between people but between abstractions: past and present, proposition and counterproposition.

As both knowledge and social relationships reconstitute through the codification of texts, an individual's social participation at once grows wider but more abstract and more conditioned by the nature of what is written. For instance, people are united by law but the unity is based on anonymity. Laws (as well as religious precepts or bureaucratic procedures) become more generalized and conventionalized. They are meant to refer to no particular citizen or no particular set of circumstances but to embrace people in their highly stylized roles as members under the law. Literate people begin to see at least part of themselves in terms of the roles that are inscribed for them in written texts, roles (and hence being) that must be interpreted on the basis of what is delineated in written texts. Writing, as it abstracts, records, and regulates social processes, shines back to literate people their own abstraction, their existence as being written. This social abstraction or anonymity pertains not only to receivers or readers of texts but to those who compose them as well. Bureaucrats, for instance, write as functionaries, as nobodies in particular. As Goody observes, "writing represents not only a method of communication at a distance but a means of distancing oneself from communication" (*Logic* 50).

In Goody's cataloging of the social changes that writing brings we see a familiar motif in strong-text accounts of literate impact—a view of writing as a rather self-fueled force that ruptures from the world of things and settings, reorganizes experience, and then gives it back to people, transformed beyond any original reckoning. Writing not only carries out the business of life but somehow carries life off, to other planes, where things start working according to a different set of rules, rules intrinsic to writing itself.

Walter J. Ong and literate cognition. Ong works some of the same territory as Goody, interested as he is in historical periods of preliteracy and literate conversion. But whereas Goody looks back in order to trace the proliferation of what are now familiar aspects of modern literate existence, Ong's gaze remains on the past and the nearly unimaginable Now of primary orality. That is, Ong's explorations of literacy are designed to explain why it is so hard for us, as late literates, to fathom adequately enough what life is like without the technology of writing.

Whereas Goody primarily focuses on the impact of writing on large social structures, Ong investigates its impact on cognitive structures—

how written language and especially print get "personally interiorized" within individuals (*Orality and Literacy* 56). For Ong, the circumstances of the acts of reading or writing carry strong teleological significance. Oral communication is communal, collective. Writing and reading are physically solitary.[2] Thus, the latter are essentially private, self-conscious acts. Reading and writing, according to Ong, "throw the psyche back on itself" (*Orality and Literacy* 69). Just as writing estranges writer from reader, it also estranges language from language users and knowledge from context. Words are alone in a text, he says, and consequently acquire status as "things" rather than "events" ("Reading" 184). Writing, he says, "divides and distances, and it divides and distances all sorts of things in all sorts of ways" ("Writing Restructures Thought" 36).

We see in Ong's descriptions of the literate condition unmistakable associations with the modern condition: alienation, anonymity, skepticism, a kind of stony, interiorized objectivity and fragmentation. All of these attitudes appear to originate in the modern's commitment to print. That is, as we commit more of our social enterprise to print, we also become committed cognitively to the outlooks that print encourages. The sheer engagement in literate practices induces this modern sensibility.

For Ong, as well as for Goody, strong text originates in the power of writing as a technology. Ong makes much of the technological nature of literacy and its unique penetration of human consciousness. Writing is a technology, first, because it requires tools—instruments for recording and disseminating. It is also a technology because it manipulates and transforms nature. It allows us to interpret nature on our terms instead of on its terms by wresting language out of oral, real-world contexts and making it a tool for contemplation of alternate worlds. Ong would concur with Goody's depiction of literacy as "the technology of the intellect" (Goody, "Introduction" 4), an unnatural intrusion into human thought. Once inside us, though, writing becomes a second nature that unleashes human potential in unprecedented ways. "More than any other single invention," Ong observes, "writing has transformed human consciousness" (*Orality and Literacy* 78).

To sum up, then, Ong concentrates his oral-literate contrast on the physical and noetic differences in the circumstances of speaking and writing: the new relationship to language, knowledge, and others that writing insists upon. The physical circumstances of writing and reading become emblems for the drastic social and cognitive disengagement and reorganization that literacy demands.

Deborah Tannen and the involvement-message continuum. It may seem strange for followers of orality-literacy debates to see Tannen's name in among strong dichotomists, for her work has been dedicated to dismantling stark orality-literacy contrasts. Tannen has advocated that orality and literacy be treated as a continuum of orientations that intermingle in everyday language use ("Oral-Literate"). For Tannen, the oral and the literate represent different channels of discourse, and any particular instance of discourse, no matter what its mode, will use a ratio of both. As Tannen points out, some people's talk sounds like books while other people's writing looks like talk (*Conversational Style*). So notions of orality and literacy stretch beyond any useful distinctions.

In fact, in her most recent work, Tannen has abandoned the terms "oral" and "literate" altogether, preferring instead a distinction between "involvement-focus" and "message-focus" or even "relative reliance on involvement focus" ("Relative Focus" 126). This shift in terminology looks beyond the mere form of a discourse (spoken or written) to characterize it on the basis of its primary channel of elaboration. Involvement-focus, according to Tannen, "carries a metamessage of rapport" and "communicates that the speaker wants to be involved with the addressee" ("Relative Focus" 125). A written text can be involvement-focused, Tannen says, to the extent to which it relies on a reader to supply background knowledge or refers to the presence of writer or reader. Message-focus, on the other hand, focuses attention on ideas and content, the aboutness of the discourse. Message-focused discourse is explicit about its message, spelling everything out for a reader with little reference to writer or reader. Rather than refer to participants, message-focused discourse will more typically refer to itself, making it more self-sufficient and impersonal and giving it the potential to mean the same thing to many people no matter where and when and by whom it is read.

Although Tannen introduces welcome complications into oral-literate contrasts, her distinctions maintain the classic underlying categories of the oral-like and the literate-like. They originate in the obvious physical differences that accompany occasions of speaking and listening versus writing and reading. Speakers look at each other; writers and readers look at a page. Speakers are oriented together in one collaborative, real-time present. Writer and reader share neither space nor time and must collaborate together alone. Moreover and most important to this distinction, speakers have para-textual resources (voice, gesture, touch, the scaffold of the dialogue, and the things in a setting) that can take the pressure off any one individual speaker's language. Without those resources, writer and reader have only words and their knowledge of and trust in language-on-its-own. Less important to each other, writer and reader become less relevant to each other. So, in typical expository discourse, the interpersonal channel is muted while the message channel is loaded.

While Tannen changes the terms of the discussion, message, in its need to be lexicalized, remains identified with the literate-like, the textual. Involvement remains identified with the oral-like. According to Tannen, no matter what the particular mode of the discourse, to signal involvement is always to arouse the oral-like context. To convey message is to arouse the literate-like context. Her formula displaces the formal oral-literate dichotomy but replaces it with an involvement-message seesaw. As we shall see in a later chapter, however, the involvement-message distinction becomes untenable from the perspectives of writers and readers in action, for whom message *is* involvement.

David R. Olson and "The Literate Bias of Schooling." The work of educational psychologist David R. Olson blends social, cognitive, and linguistic perspectives but reformulates them more specifically around the unusual literacy demands of schooling. Schools have the social mission to prepare students for eventual roles in modern literate domains, to make them able to function in technological and bureaucratic systems. So the primary goal of the school is to produce socially functional literates. But it is also true that the means of learning in school are texts. To *become* literates, students very quickly have to *be* literate. The devastating impact of early reading failure in school attests to this unusual means-ends relationship within the context of school literacy. Both the means and ends of literacy take important places in Olson's treatments of oral-literate differences.

For Olson, oral-literate contrasts are interpreted above all in terms of the transition between home and school. What changes, he asks, must children undergo as they leave the emotionally charged, familiar, and essentially oral world of the household and step into the literate realm of the school, where even oral language primarily serves to reinforce an orientation to the printed word? Like other strong-text advocates, Olson sees the transition as requiring a dramatic repudiation of the interpretive habits of everyday discourse in favor of the new and different demands of the text ("The Language of Instruction").

According to Olson, the everyday discourse that young children are involved in at home is interpersonally based: the status of the speaker is intertwined with the message and thereby intertwined with the meaning of the message. Olson says children learn language initially not in terms of what words say but in terms of the actions and results words bring about. Children comprehend language in terms of its pragmatic function. But in explicit written discourse, particularly in school textbooks, the social relationship of writer to reader and the relationship of writer to message are irrelevant to the making of meaning. "It is this social or pragmatic aspect of meaning," Olson writes, "which appears to be altered, if not obliterated, when we turn from the oral language of conversation to the written languages of the texts used in school" ("Social Aspects" 101). Textbook language is virtually bereft of illocutionary markers, Olson points out. The language carries few indicators of social relationships and human intentions; rather, as a form of archival language, the language of textbooks appears as a series of disembodied assertions, impersonal and authoritative. It is, in Tannen's terms, sheer message.

In various essays, Olson describes the fundamental interpretive shift that must occur when intention drops out and written meaning goes it alone. In some cases he describes it as an ascendancy of the "logical" function of language over the "rhetorical" or "social" ("From Utterance to Text"). In other cases he sees it as a difference between the "casual" meaning of oral discourse and the "literal" meaning of written discourse (Olson and Hildyard). That is, in spoken exchanges we tend to privilege the world at the expense of words: we adjust our interpretation of someone's spoken words to what we know about the world and what we think the speaker really means to say. The exact words do not matter so much, and, in fact, are often quickly forgotten. But in written discourse, the reverse tends to be true, according to Olson. We privilege language over the world and are more apt to adjust our understanding to the literal text. In written discourse, the exact words do matter. We align our understanding of what a text means with our understanding of what a text says, because a text (when it is working right) says what it means and means what it says. This process results in "literal" meaning. Like Tuman, Olson sees this potential to adjust the world to the word as a big advantage of literacy because it allows the exploration of "possible worlds," by which language can work against the pressures of intuition and commonsense reality to make something else the case.

Olson's formulation of the "literate bias" also serves as a diagnosis of early school success and failure. According to Olson, children from print-reliant households develop a textual orientation long before they even actually start to read or write—an orientation carried in the oral language of literate groups. They learn early that language can be treated opaquely, as a system for manipulation, and they learn early to treat words as separate from people, worthy of interpretation in their own right. In a way, he says, children from literacy-reliant homes are literate long before they begin formal instruction. Children from less literacy-oriented households may not learn such an orientation in their early oral years. For them, an awareness of language as language will have to be a consequence of learning to read. They will have, in that sense, a longer row to hoe when they get to school (" 'See! Jumping!' ").

Olson's descriptions emphasize parallel transitions from home to school and "from utterance to text." Learning to read and learning to go to school are metaphors for each other. Both require an unmooring from one's local social groundings to handle decontextualized symbols in decontextualized circumstances. To be a reader and to succeed in school, one must enter—and be able to enter—the house of language-on-its-own.

Underlying Assumptions in Strong-Text Literacy

Although strong-text theorists approach literacy from different perspectives and with different interests, they share a view of the text as the centripetal power in literacy development. Look closely at what makes texts textual, they argue, and there you will find the stuff of literacy. "Writing" in the work of Goody and Ong, especially, refers to textual inscriptions, rather than to the acts or activities of people writing. For them it is writing as artifact that presents the major puzzles. Ong and Goody also start their cultural inquiries retroactively, working backward from the results and aftermaths (i.e., products) of the so-called literate revolution. Even scholars who give more attention to questions of how discourse is produced, such as Tannen or Olson, tend to focus on the surface features of finished pieces of discourse as a basis for characterizing literacy. Olson, for instance, uses transcripts of the speech of low- and high-ability young readers to demonstrate what he sees as the latter group's literate tendency to treat language objectively. That is, he treats features in the surface of their discourse (a product) as a cause for their success as readers (Torrance and Olson; Olson "Writing").

To understand why the text is so central in these formulations it is necessary to see that for strong-text theorists literacy is best understood as a technology, a penetrating force that unnaturalizes and reorganizes all that it comes in contact with. The phonetic alphabet figures importantly in the formulations of Goody, Ong, and Olson as the technological breakthrough that precipitated literacy. They describe the alphabet as the means by which language could pull free from the limitations of crude semiotic marks and localized meaning to achieve autonomous representation. Pictures and other forms of icons or indexes could only gesture out to the shared world as it is, could only point the interpreter somewhere else in the present time and the real world to infer meaning. The alphabet, arbitrary, regular, exacting, and opaque, calls attention to itself instead. It says, "Look here." The alphabet is the origin of the centripetal powers that strong-text theories ascribe to written language. It supplies the lift-off that brings the other two important qualities of strong text: autonomy and anonymity.

Autonomy. Autonomy relates to the sheer mundane materiality of written language. Written language can be called autonomous because it can be differentiated as an entity in the world. It can be called autonomous because it exists, as inscription, independently from the physical presence and even living existence of its author. Autonomous written language can last longer than its author and longer than any particular reader. Its potential resides in its permanent outline on a page.

But this seemingly simple detachment of language from breath brings with it, in the strong-text view, a host of changes that are far from mundane. The detachability and preservability of language are seen, in Goody's work, to foster the rise of the modern bureaucratic society. They also engender what Karl Popper calls the "third world" of objective knowledge, knowledge, as he puts it, "without a knowing subject" (109). Objective knowledge is human thought made into object and turned out into the world, coming back around to influence the state of affairs in the world. "Autonomy" as a concept in strong-text theories does not mean that written language can utterly transcend social context, but it does mean that written language comes to have its own status in the social context. It becomes the bargaining agent in literate exchanges of meaning.

To function as this arbiter, according to strong-text theories, written language draws to itself elaborate negotiating powers of grammar and syntax, powers that serve to stabilize and conventionalize meaning. Written language usurps and fixes into its structures much of the otherwise diffuse and ad hoc meaning that wafts around in typical talk.[3] Structure becomes meaning. Definitions are set down in dictionaries, which are another means of arbitration. The absorption of meaning into

stable written conventions breaks reliance upon situational context—
written language can mean the same thing regardless of time and setting.
From there it it a short step to anonymity.

Anonomity. Like autonomy, anonymity takes on linguistic, cognitive,
and social significance in strong-text accounts. Linguistically, it translates
into Tannen's idea of message-focus, the ascendancy of the what over
the who. For Ong, it is the inescapable "gaps" and "absences" of literate
experience, registering at once the awful loss of first orality and the
liberation into private, idiosyncratic revelry that writers and readers
enjoy ("Reading" 173). Anonymity is the functional status of Goody's
bureaucratic literate and, in Olson's formulations, the state in which
school book-learning takes place.

Also like autonomy, anonymity begins as a mundane fact of material
texts, a fact which then precipitates new forms of social relationships
among literates. Anonymous written language rises as a kind of wall
between writer and reader, a third presence that does not exist in talk.
As a result, we are said to deal not directly with each other in literate
exchanges but deal, on this side or the other, with language. Alignment
of consciousness in writing and reading is not with the other but with
the language on the page.

The anonymity that, in strong-text accounts, comes with the liberation
of language from breath also brings liberation from the restricted capacity of oral speech merely to express or signal, that is, to remain affiliated
with the speaker. With written discourse arise the objectified and objectifying language functions of description and argumentation. These new
capacities, as Popper has explored, free discourse from being merely a
running commentary on life-as-it-is and allows it to become a tool of
theory, a means of dissection, criticism, and speculation (106–52). This
is an important consequence, in strong-text formulations. Language not
only becomes detachable and preservable but becomes available for
representing experience in ways other than we apprehend it phenome-
nologically. Written language rises as a potentially resistant force, capa-
ble of altering time, space, and commonsense perception through the
powers of its own inherent logic. Written texts develop their own voice,
outside of us, referring not to the known world but to themselves and
to each other.

Literacy as textuality. It is clear from the foregoing discussion that
strong-text theorists focus their investigations of literacy on the characteristics of texts. The artifact of the written text manifests both the
requisites and repercussions of literacy. Because texts are physically

decontextualized pieces of language, decontextualization comes to be seen as the essential interpretive move that literacy requires. Because texts are abstract objects, conceptual, logical, literal, and detached, so too does literacy come to be characterized in the same terms—either to say that these are the cognitive attitudes one needs to approach texts or that these are the cognitive attitudes that texts bequeath to individuals who "deal" with them.

This equivalence of literacy with textuality also makes separation, in the strong-text view, the most salient aspect of literate experience. The alphabet, a set of discrete phonetic tools, pries language from "the lifeworld" and offers it back to people for analysis. This separation triggers still more separation: of self as object of consciousness and of discourse domains as discrete spheres of activity. The "third world" of autonomous textual knowledge asserts itself as a separate force of development.

Social separation is also the major theme in descriptions of individual literacy. It appears as the first key interpretive move than enables literacy growth in school: the separation of child from home, language from action. More broadly, the physical and temporal distance of writer and reader, while provoking a functional need for literacy, becomes an occasion for psychological escape—an opportunity for writer and reader to revel, alone, in language, alone, unfettered by social cooperation. That is why, in Myron Tuman's estimation, to write is to engage in "a fundamental act of social betrayal" (32).

Oral-Literate Blendings in Strong-Text Models of Literacy

Theories of literacy derived from oral-literate contrasts have been vulnerable to criticism from many quarters, primarily for their tendency to depict literacy as a monolithic technology with predictable social and cognitive consequences. In *The Psychology of Literacy,* Scribner and Cole offer a painstaking critique of the assertion that literacy intrinsically promotes such cognitive habits as abstract reasoning. They demonstrate that many of the cognitive consequences attributed to literacy are actually effects of schooling and that whatever consequences literacy brings will be a result of the social practices with which it is associated. What literacy does to you, in other words, depends on what you do with it. Shirley Brice Heath's *Ways with Words* also explores the plurality of literacies even among social groups who may have common school experiences. Her study demonstrates that the practices and very meanings of literacy are of a piece with a social group's orientation to time, space, problem-solving, child-rearing, storytelling, and other social arrangements. Her descriptions of the collective, improvisational nature of reading on the porches and in the churches of a black, working-class community in the Carolina Piedmont, for instance, challenges the Ongian association of reading with social and psychic isolation.

Other critics, notably Brian Street, have focused on the ideological and political foundations of various characterizations of literacy. A dominant social group will elevate its brand of literacy to the status of Literacy, marking other versions as deviant or "restricted." For instance, in "Restricted Literacy in Northern Ghana," Goody argued that literacy associated with religion tends to restrict the potential power of literacy, which he associates with independent, even democratic thought. The secrecy surrounding magical religions, the tendency for holy books to be preserved in nonvernacular languages, and the high premium placed on obedience to "the word" all suppress the potentially liberating powers of secular literacies, according to Goody.[4] But, Street maintains that affiliating literacy with democracy, secular reasoning, logic, detachment, and categorical thinking is merely a means of promoting a system of elitist, Western practices and values. What the critiques of Scribner and Cole, Heath, Street, and others have in common is skepticism toward a standard or monolithic portrayal of literacy and its effects in favor of more cultural, contextual, and political interpretations. (For other recent critiques, see Pattison; also Rose's "Narrowing the Mind and Page.")

While these criticisms and revisions are important and well taken, it should be observed that strong-text theorists do acknowledge the many "interfaces" and "overlappings" of the oral and the literate and, at times, modulate their claims about the unique impact of Western literacy. Ong notices, for instance, that despite the revolutionary consequences of the "radically decontextualizing mechanism" of writing, it maintains meaning only in relationship to the spoken word ("Writing Restructures Thought" 39). Thus the distancing that literacy inspires "is not total or permanent, for every reading of a text consists of restoring it, directly or indirectly, to sound, vocally or in the imagination." He also observes that while textuality separates the knower from the known, that separation too is only temporary. Knowledge ultimately resides only in the living human being who reanimates text-based knowledge "more consciously and more articulately" as a result of literacy ("Writing Restructures Thought" 48).

Jack Goody, particularly in his most recent work, downplays the strict oral-literate dichotomies, both cultural and cognitive, that many critics thought marked his earlier formulations.[5] *The Interface Between the Written and the Oral,* published in 1987, traces the gradual penetration of literacy into existing oral traditions and offers corrections to prevailing misconceptions about the nature of "oral" memory. Goody also softens his earlier characterization of the Greek phonetic alphabet, seeing it less as an unprecedented, revolutionary breakthough and more in a multicultural continuum of developing written scripts. Goody also is more cautious about ascribing inevitable cognitive consequences to the acquisition of literacy and quicker to acknowledge the logic of nonliterate thinking (although he still regards syllogistic logic as a distinctly literate invention). He calls for a less strictly cognitive perspective on the nature and impact of literacy and advocates more cultural, Vygotskian perspectives.

Deborah Tannen, who, as was noted, has been the most resistant to automatic oral-literate dichotomizing, suggests that the "involvement focus" associated with oral communication plays a role in reading and writing. She observes:

> A particularly fascinating aspect of the notion of involvement- and information-focused strategies is the possibility that the former, which have been associated with spoken language, may be the most efficient for both writing and reading. ... The ability to imagine what a hypothetical reader needs to know is an interactive skill. ... [Similarly] good readers use highly context-sensitive skills, strategies that I am suggesting are interactive or involvement-focused. ("Relative Focus" 140)

David R. Olson offers yet another dimension to oral-literate blendings when he suggests that literate orientation is passed in the "objectifying" talk between literate parents and their young children. Thus, he sees the involvement-focused settings of parent-child conversation (especially conversation around print) as a site for training in message-focus.

All in all we would have to say, then, that strong-text accounts of literacy attempt various reconciliations of the oral and the literate— although seeing them, nevertheless, as antagonistic interpretive stances.

In some cases this reconciliation takes the form of acknowledging the influence of cultural contexts and the oral "lifeworld" in shaping literacy and its outcomes. In other cases it is a matter of depicting literalism, decontextualism, autonomy of meaning, and abstraction of thought merely as literate *tendencies,* more the ideal goals of the alphabetic code than actual achievements of it. In yet other cases, the oral and the literate appear as simultaneous strands or forces present in varying proportions in all forms of literate language use—making literate development somehow a mixture of the two.

The controversy over the cognitive consequences of literacy is not within the scope of this study. Nor is my goal to show how context continues to "taint" literate language and literate enterprises no matter how far they may strain for decontextualization (or for the mere appearance of it). Rather, my aim is to argue that this whole framework—a framework that puts the literate in tension with the oral, the message in tension with involvement, and the text in tension with context—is the wrong framework for thinking about reading and writing and the nature of literacy. Strong-text models may account at some level for the potential of literacy—that is, they may account for what writing makes possible as a technology that oral language does not. But that is not the same thing as establishing what makes possible the human acts of writing and reading. To the extent to which we look to "strong text" as an explanation for the latter question, we are barking up the wrong tree.

Context, Reference, and Meaning in Writing and Reading: Toward a Process Account of Literacy

As we have seen, the oral-literate dichotomy rests on a dichotomized relationship of context and text, a relationship that is said to undergo a fundamental shift between the oral and the literate. In speech, the direction of meaning is from context to text; in writing and reading, it is from text to context. Initially this is an extremely plausible and comprehensive explanation. It accounts, at a basic level, for the fact that speakers "have" a context (a real-world, present-tense, mutually reliable setting) that writer and reader do not have. It explains how semantic context—a world of words—rushes in to sustain literate exchanges. It seems to account for the obvious linguistic differences between typical spoken and written discourse. It explains the power of text to create new worlds. And it offers a theory of literacy development as a growing ability to accomplish this shift in interpretive direction: to rely on language as the controlling agent in meaning, rather than the world of people, places, and things. But this explanation rests on the erroneous assumption that context and language are separate entities, separate sources of meaning.

Before taking up that point, it will be necessary to explore the several meanings of "context" that usually inform discussions of the oral and the literate. The usual meaning is something like "situation" or "setting" or what Ong calls "lifeworld," encompassing ordinary elements of reality like time, space, manifest objects and conditions, ongoing activity, and the joint presence of participants with recognized social roles. From such a concrete definition speaking can be characterized as "reliant" on context, while writing and reading can be characterized as proceeding in the "absence" of context or as abstracted from context. Olson and Hildyard have defined context rather more elegantly as the "possible world" that a particular text relates to or in which a text would find sense ("Writing and Literal Meaning"). In oral exchanges, usually, the "possible world" is the ordinary, taken-for-granted social world while in literate exchanges the "possible world" often tends to be a stipulated text world, a world that a text explicates into existence. This definition broadens context beyond an immediate physical setting to incorporate, at least potentially, such things as beliefs, customs, and history.

Other definitions of context identify it more strictly as the shared backgrounds of participants that can be invoked when needed during an exchange. Context here is more clearly a mental construct, something Edwards and Mercer in *Common Knowledge* define as "everything that the participants in a conversation know and understand, over and above that which is explicit in what they say, that contributes to how they make sense of what is said" (63). This definition readily accommodates knowledge of procedural rules and routines that figure in speech-act theory and other pragmatic accounts of language use and meaning. Through a strong-text lens, typical oral exchanges appear to rely relatively more heavily on existing shared knowledge of immediate participants while, in typical literate exchanges, shared background knowledge is established by the text (in other words, the implicit backgrounds of literate exchanges have to be explicitly constructed).

Whether a physical situation or a mental construct, however, context tends to be construed in these treatments as something separate from language, so that either language occurs "in" a context or a context is made "out of" language. I want to argue, though, along with ethnomethodologist Rolf Kjolseth, that:

> A grasp of accomplished, natural language cannot be won by focusing on either language or context. Each is barren, and both only take on substance when we inquire into the interactive phenomenon of understanding when they flow together into the ongoing accomplishment of social realities. In that accomplishment . . . is an occurrent social structure brought to life by its members. (50)

Kjolseth recognizes that all language use proceeds from a broad sense of "what is going on here," and that language and context mutually and inextricably constitute each other. To use and understand language requires knowing how to accomplish language *and* its setting simultaneously, knowing how to use language not merely to share meaning with others but also to constitute the conditions necessary for meaning to be shared.[6] What specific changes in perspective are brought about when we see context as an embodiment of language and language as an embodiment of context?

First, classic distinctions between oral and literate contexts are undermined. Even in oral exchanges context is always an accomplishment of the participants, not a given. Meaning is not already there to be relied upon but must be made and remade, minute by accomplished minute, through people's particular interchanges and interpretations. The actual context of any language act are the socially forged conditions of mutual awareness through which private understandings can be shared with others. In that sense meaning in oral exchanges is as much the pure product of words as meaning in literate exchanges. Both types of exchange require participants to establish and sustain, through language, an ongoing, publicly accomplished sense of "what is going on here" by which meaning can be constituted. The "what is going on here" in textual language are the unfolding acts of writing and reading: those dynamic settings of action must be mutually sustained as part of a writer's and reader's sense of the text.

This puts intersubjectivity (the mutual recognition of the presence of the other) at the core of interpretation and meaning in literate as well as oral exchanges. Writer and reader are together in that they are, at any moment, at the same "place" in a text, a right-here, right-now social reality of their mutual making. As a text unfolds, this joint history of shared place forms the context for what is to follow. Textual language finds meaning within this common lived experience, this developing history of "the we who are involved here." Thus, although literate texts may be vehicles to the alternate worlds of fiction, theory, or social resistance, those worlds are constituted and sustained in the collaborative involvement of writer and reader—the same kind of cooperative, interpretive-working involvement that keeps our ordinary social world afloat.

In what specific ways does this perspective challenge strong-text explanations? Recall that strong-text proponents rely crucially on the notion of separation of language from social context as central to literate interpretation and consciousness. They stress not only the obvious independence from situation that material inscription achieves but also the power of the material text to pull its language apart (at least temporarily) from its own context, to "delay," as Tuman says, the fusion of what is said with what is meant, to disengage semantic relationships from social ones. Heightened consciousness of this momentary separation becomes, for Olson, the impetus for literalism (and, for deconstructionists, the impetus for endless play in the gap). But this explanation assumes an abdication of the grounds of intersubjectivity as the basis of reference in written language.[7] I am suggesting that these grounds are not abdicated but rather claimed with a vengeance during writing and reading. The heightened consciousness that writing brings *is* consciousness of intersubjectivity as the basis of reference in all language use. Writing pulls into sharp focus the means by which we make the world together.

This argument is developed in the following chapters, first by looking closely at some writers at work, exploring the dynamic contexts of action in which they compose and how their emerging texts function to help constitute those contexts. A look at the writing process of one expert writer, especially, will demonstrate how textual language refers not merely to an ostensible text world under construction but to the writer's here-and-now working context, including his awareness of the presence of the other. Later chapters will reapproach typical expository texts with insights that a process-perspective makes available. To see what is cognitively going on around a text as it is being written or read is to appreciate how much textual language is *about* those goings on, how it carries constant reference to what writer and reader are doing together.

This change in perspective allows a reassessment of standard, "message-focused" expository written texts as, in fact, highly metacommunicative and involvement-focused: outcomes of a thickening history of "the we."

Such a process perspective on writing, reading, and texts argues against an equivalence of literacy with textuality (at least as textually is typically defined) because it places one's involvement with other people—rather than with texts—at the center of literate interpretation and development. As we have seen, strong-text theories model literacy as the way of the text. The text as object—opaque, autonomous, and anonymous—is said to reflect the underlying attitudes and stances that literacy entails. But if we see literacy as a growing metacommunicative ability—an increasing awareness of and control over the social means by which people sustain discourse, knowledge, and reality—then social involvement becomes the key model for literacy and literacy growth. This involvement takes several forms. Specifically, making sense of print requires the fundamental realization that written language is about an involvement of writer and reader; its reference and meaning depend on the intersubjective bonds established in the acts of writing and reading. Developmentally, that makes knowledge about the acts of reading and writing—why and how people accomplish these acts—the key knowledge for literacy development. Learning to read and write depends critically on immediate social involvements with people who read and write and who can show you how the work goes. More broadly, this perspective suggests that we look toward our ordinary social ties with others not as retrogressive barriers to literate transcendence but as the very means that enable reading and writing and the very essence of literate reflection.

These latter issues—and their implications for rethinking literacy success and failure in school—will be the subject of Chapter Five. Now we turn to a consideration of writing and reading processes. When the focus moves from product to process—from strong text to people actually accomplishing acts of writing and reading—descriptions of literate experience change significantly. Rather than subsiding, "context," "involvement," and "metacommunication" surge forward as central concerns. A process perspective demands a new vocabulary for thinking and talking about literacy and offers new possibilities for reapproaching some of our most pressing literacy problems.

Chapter Two

"What Now?" The Processes of Involvement

In 1971 Janet Emig published *The Composing Processes of Twelfth Graders,* a set of eight case studies in which she asked her adolescent subjects, among other things, to think aloud as they composed two essays, saying everything that was going through their minds as they planned, drafted, revised, and edited their writing. Although not the first research to attend to composing processes, Emig's monograph became the watershed for what is called "the process movement" in composing research and teaching.[1] As a pedagogical initiative "process" emphasizes a shift away from a focus on finished texts as objects of analysis and imitation toward the more practical questions of how people do the behind-the-scenes work of writing. Process pedagogy, which puts high value on invention, revision, and peer and teacher response during drafting stages, has changed the character of writing instruction in schools and colleges in the United States.

As a research initiative, the process perspective has led in the past ten years to more systematic investigations of the cognition of writing. Perhaps the most systematic explorations of the mental activity of composing have been undertaken by Linda Flower and John R. Hayes at Carnegie-Mellon University. They have collected scores of oral (think aloud) protocols from experienced and less experienced adult writers. From protocol research, Flower and Hayes have developed a "cognitive process theory of writing" that depicts writing as a goal-directed and highly dynamic thinking process consisting of recursive cycles of planning, drafting, and reviewing. They also have provided portraits of writers-at-work that point up sharp contrasts in the procedures of "experts" and "novices."

Flower and Hayes' project has met with criticism from Marilyn Cooper and Michael Holzman, among others, for its intrusive oral-protocol methodology and for the artificial laboratory conditions of the early experiments.[2] The project also has been faulted by Patricia Bizzell in "Cognition, Convention, and Certainty" and, more recently, by Martin Nystrand, among others, for neglecting the role of social context in shaping written discourse. Flower and Hayes' cognitive-process theory treats the individual, isolated writer as the originator of goals and plans for writing with little consideration of how those mental constructions relate to a wider discourse community or even to the public language of a developing text. Understanding what writers do when they compose, critics argue, requires a wider view of both writers' social identities and the cultural resources and constraints that they contend with. Because social and cultural assumptions are so often unconscious, they will fall below the threshhold of articulation in oral protocol reports. They also will not be easily accommodated in a model of composing so narrowly focused on the individual mind as the origin of action and meaning in composing.

Despite these very serious drawbacks, I would like to try to retrieve the "cognitive process" of composing as an important site for deepening understanding about the nature of literacy. While Flower and Hayes' theoretical model holds little interest here, because of the limitations just cited, the actual data of oral protocols are of intriguing value because of the window they provide into the dynamic character of literacy in action. However multifaceted literacy is, its many components converge when a writer starts to write or a reader starts to read. Any truly comprehensive and realistic definition of literacy must take into account the actual acts of reading and writing, must take into account, in other words, how literacy is actually accomplished by everyday readers and writers in everyday life. While intrusive and incomplete, oral protocols still provide a singularly rich record of the minute-by-minute accomplishments of written meaning making and thus stand to enlarge existing conceptions of literacy and literate ability.

Oral protocols also are potentially rich records of the social contexts of writing and reading, providing social context is not construed as an external, reified force but as something that writer or reader is accomplishing as part of the act of composing or comprehending. As I argued in the previous chapter, we make social reality, including social structure, over and over again in the interactions and interpretations in which we are engaged. Because social context is always an accomplishment of language and cognition, it should be available for view in think-aloud records, if we learn how to look for it. Arguments that pit the social against the cognitive as if the two are like oil and water overlook that the social is in the cognitive and the cognitive is in the social, as the two "flow together," as Kjolseth says, "into the ongoing accomplishment of social realities" (50). In language use especially the inextricability of the social and the cognitive must be recognized and accounted for.

So my fundamental aim in this chapter is to articulate the important messages about the social nature of literacy that come from a cognitive-process perspective on writing and reading, especially as it invites rethinking of strong-text characterizations. Of special interest will be differences that are emerging in pictures of effective versus less effective writers-at-work (and their parallels with effective and less effective readers). These comparisons offer a compelling occasion for thinking about what is actually growing when we talk about literacy growth. As this chapter will argue, literate development seems to entail a growing ability to see a kind of double meaning in written language: an ability to see not merely what a text is saying but what it is saying about you, that is, what it is saying about what you need to be doing next as a writer or a reader. Expert writers and readers seem able to see this kind of metacommunicative meaning in written language while inexperienced or ineffective writers and readers miss it. This contrast will be developed by looking at oral protocols by two writers, one of them an expert, to trace how they accomplish context as part of the act of composing and how text language finds metacommunicative reference as part of this context of action. We also will look at the role of reading during writing as a means for sustaining context.

First, though, to the general contributions that a process perspective can make to an understanding of literacy.

From Product to Process: Exploring the Nature of Literate Acts

One of the most useful innovations of process inquiry is that it takes literacy off the seesaw with orality and treats it on its own terms. As a result, literate experience returns to time and place. The technologies of alphabet and print freeze language onto paper, making it available for transport and preservation. But writing (or reading) is a here-and-now enterprise, always occurring in the present tense. It unfolds as a cognitive process as evanescent as speech, erased and usually forgotten in the act of being accomplished. While research indicates that readers have somewhat better recall of "the very words" of a text than listeners do of "the very words" of conversation, process research shows how writers and readers easily forget the routes they have taken to arrive at "the very words" and their meaning. Flower and Hayes, for instance, report that when writers are "debriefed" following protocol sessions, they frequently cannot recall many of the local, interim goals and plans that they articulated during composing. The local plans and goals are forgotten once accomplished. A process perspective emphasizes the evanescent accomplishments of literate meaning-making.

Other important innovations mark the process approach in writing research. Process accounts make a break with the material qualities of a text as a basis for explaining acts of writing. Prior to the work of Flower and Hayes, even so-called process models of writing maintained a conceptual affiliation with the text. An act of writing was seen to evolve in the same way a text visibly does. Writing was described as a series of steps or stages, from prewriting (to correlate with the before-text), to drafting (the text), to revising and editing.[3] Flower and Hayes shifted the basis of explanation. Acknowledging that a text is indeed an evolving product in an act of writing (although, interestingly, not the only product), their inquiry went deeper, to seek the constituent thinking processes that underwrite the evolution. They asked, essentially, not how a text is made but rather what is going on as a text is made.

What they found was that cycles of planning, reviewing, and revising, both global and local, erupt throughout a writing process, inspired by an array of exigencies, not just the demands for a well-formed text. The "pregnant pauses" of writing do not often correlate with natural breaks in a text, such as sections or paragraphs, but relate more often to high-level rhetorical designing, which can occur at any time ("Pregnant Pause"). Flower and Hayes' windows into the composing process reveal a kind of multimedia event, a congestion of nonverbal plans, images, loose ends, dead ends, private labels, as well as the public language of the evolving text ("Images, Plans, Prose").

This same concern with process over product shaped their inquiry into the differences between expert and novice writers. Instead of seeking obvious differences in the qualities of texts the two groups might produce, Flower and Hayes sought to detect significant differences in what the two groups do during the course of writing. This is an especially important conceptual break for approaches to literacy because it says, in effect, that the essence of literacy (cultural or cognitive) is not available for view in a finished text. Rather, it is best approached in terms of experiences and know-how that people develop and harness. To understand what is growing when we talk about literacy growth, we must look not at textual "hardware" (vocabularly, syntax, organizational and rhetorical patterns, levels of abstraction, and other textual evidence) but at the means and methods of writers (and readers) at work. Although too often this has translated into crude quantitative comparisons (i.e., good writers write "more" and revise "more" than poorer ones), the conceptual framework nevertheless poses an important challenge to prevailing text-centered definitions (and assessments) of literacy.[4]

The portraits that Flower and Hayes have drawn of expert and novice writers also pose an interesting challenge to text-centered characterizations of literacy. According to Olson and others, the transformation from the oral to the literate requires accepting the "obliteration" of pragmatic meaning as a basis for interpretation. Yet, the single differentiating mark of effective writers is their awareness of and ability to exploit pragmatic meaning in the process of composing—not only for readers but for themselves. And it is the inability of ineffective writers to attend to pragmatic implications of their language that often leads to a breakdown in composing. As Flower and Hayes have described (and other studies corroborate), effective writers spend a majority of their time and attention during writing on representing to themselves a situation at hand.[5] They work from a mixture of "to do" plans, which relate to the intended rhetorical and structural accomplishments of the public text; "to say" plans, which carry out "to do" plans; and process or composing plans, by which a writer organizes the entire event that is under way ("Dynamics of Composing"). Whereas poorer writers focus mostly on "to say" plans (especially what to say next), effective writers focus more on global "to do" plans and process plans ("Cognition of Discovery"). This same profile emerges in studies of expert and novice readers. Effective readers are more goal-directed and, like good writers, create and maintain a network of immediate and long-range plans by which they manage and monitor their process and level of understanding. On the other hand, just as poor writers tend to focus narrowly on what to say next, poor readers tend to focus only on what the text is saying next.[6]

Overall, representations of the situation-at-hand that effective writers and readers create and maintain tend to be flexible, particular, and dynamic, growing in depth and breath as an act of writing or reading unfolds. Representations by less effective writers and readers are general, static, and flat, often not changing much from beginning to end. When Flower and Hayes observe that good writers "are simply solving a different problem than poor writers" when they write ("Cognition of Discovery" 30), they mean that good writers perceive "what is going on here" in a much different way. As the ensuing discussion will demonstrate, this difference in perception holds the key to the nature of literate orientation.

Literacy as Knowing What to Do Now

Process inquiry reveals that the text, which looms as the central power in prevailing strong-text accounts of literacy, is not the central concern of writers and readers in action, especially skilled ones. Their chief concern is not "What does that say?" or "What do I make that say?" but more like, "What do I do now?" That is, the focus in writing or reading is on keeping the entire process itself going, even when—and especially when—semantic meaning may be breaking down. The challenge for writers and readers is not merely how to make a text make sense but how to make what they are doing make sense. From a process perspective we see that the essence of literate orientation is knowing what to do now.

To see writers or readers enmeshed in their work, in a dynamic context of planning, deciding, hypothesizing, darting ahead, taking back, and so on, is to see that textual language is indeed embedded in contexts of practical action—the action of writing or reading. The words take their meaning in this context, and only by staying oriented to this context can writers and readers keep making the words mean something. To put this another way we might say that meaning in written language is neither literal nor casual but rather "strategic"[7]— or what I have been calling metacommunicative. Knowing how to write or read is knowing what a text means for things on your end, knowing what it is saying about what you need to be doing, right here, right now.

This leads to two important correctives to strong-text models of literacy. First, literacy must be seen as a context-making rather than a context-breaking ability. Skilled literates pull together and maintain *situated meaning,* what Flower and Hayes have called "current meaning," as a guide in their work. As Flower and Hayes have described it, current meaning "may be a distant cousin to the meaning formulated in a finished text" ("Images, Plans, and Prose" 122). Yet it is this meaning that is in charge: from a sense of current meaning writers make the decisions that keep writing going. Current meaning does not refer to a textual context nor a semantic context nor a text world but rather to a here-and-now, off-the-page sense of what is going on.

Poor writers and readers frequently seem not to know how to set to work. For them, reading and writing *do* proceed in a kind of Ongian psychic isolation. They attempt to produce or decipher language in the absence of situation and system. They literally seem to have no place to bring the language into, no place to gather sense from, as they try to move along the surfaces of the textual language, one or so words at a time. They proceed with only a slender grasp of what is going on. This is a problem not of an overdependence on context for meaning but a lack of a viable context for meaning.

In stressing the important role of a "working" context in writing and reading, I do not mean to underestimate the influence of the text. But this brings us to the second major corrective that I think a process perspective offers to strong-text theories of literacy. Strong-text accounts stress the archival function of written texts in shaping literate experience. They assume that reading and writing take their natures from the unique functions and capacities of autonomous textual language. In the prevailing view, to write is to unleash language as a formidable third force in both cognition and social exchange. To write words down is to lose control of them, in a sense, as they take on an objective life in the realm of the detached text world. However, written texts do not only have the archival function to sustain (i.e., preserve) meaning by means of independent technology. They also have a here-and-now role in helping people sustain the work of writing and reading. From a process perspective we see that the salient question is not how reading and writing serve to maintain the institution of written language (an impression one might easily reach from reading the works of Ong, Goody, Olson, and others) but rather how written language serves the minute-by-minute acts of writing and reading. How, we must ask, do writers and readers use an evolving text to keep themselves going? And must not this function of the text be considered in characterizing literacy and literate language?

To answer this question it is first necessary to see a text not as a fixed artifact but as the public social reality (the public context) in which writing and reading unfold. To write words down is not to give them a detached life but to give them a public life—to make them shared. To commit oneself to paper is really to "give one's word" to someone else, to commit to having written something. From the perspectives of writer and reader in the act, the unfolding text represents, minute by minute, the public conditions that each can lay claim to as they go about their work. It is the spilled milk, the water over the dam, with which writer and reader—together—contend. It is the public shared context—the intersubjective situation as it stands—in which the private mental activities of writing and reading take shape and significance. Out of a mutual commitment to the "already shared," writers and readers can continue to conduct the unfolding acts of writing and reading.

Let me ground some of these contentions in the following excerpt of a think-aloud protocol by an expert writer at work.[8] (In using the general classifications of "expert" and "novice" or "effective" and "less effective," I recognize the problematic categorical assumptions behind those labels. One has to recognize the situational nature of any expertise. A so-called expert writer, placed in unfamiliar or unusually demanding circumstances, might very well start using strategies that are usually associated with novices or weak writers. Research also shows that "good" readers, asked to read texts on subjects with which they have no familiarity, will take on the profile generally reserved for "weak" readers. It is probably more accurate to see actual writers and readers as composites of expert and novice abilities. Given all these reservations, however, the categories still have had salience for me both as a teacher and a researcher. Experts are those who seem to know how to set to work as writers or readers, even when they are faced with new or unusual demands. Experts, unlike novices, maintain an unshakable faith that an act of writing or reading will yield meaning and they keep working, systematically and flexibly, to arrive at satisfactory meaning. It is left to consider exactly why and how experts are able to do that.)

At any rate, the expert writer at work in the excerpt below is a college sophomore, a nineteen-year-old, English-speaking, black, middle-class male, who was born in Guyana and has lived in Barbados, England, and the United States. He is writing an essay for an introductory composition course at the midwestern university he attends. The essay is about the so-called literacy crisis among American high-school youths and is being addressed to what the writer has decided is a "general audience." Although much could be said about this excerpt, I want to focus specifically on what the textual language means to the writer (how he sees it within the context of his work) and how the writer's constant monitoring of the intersubjective conditions (how he sees his words getting read) helps him to decide what to do next.

(The cards that the writer refers to are note cards he had been accumulating during a week of reading and discussing in class. The words that are underlined are the words that the writer is writing down. The words in quotation marks are what the writer is reading from his draft. The excerpt begins as the writer scans the opening few sentences, which he has just drafted.)

1. An introductory paragraph like that seems to suggest that
2. I'm going to talk about U.S. literacy. . . . "Today (in
3. recent years) the question of a literacy crisis has come
4. to notice in the discussions of teachers and parents of
5. students graduating in this country.". . . Maybe we can then
6. say <u>But is this a localized observation or</u> or <u>does</u> or
7. does <u>the same situation arise elsewhere?</u> . . . Now this
8. sentence is intended to allow me to get an immediate
9. handle on things . . . uh . . . How about a sentence that more
10. or less orients me. . . . This is uh something like well
11. maybe not (<u>Let's take a look</u>) but that uh general
12. idea. . . . Might as well write that. . . . <u>at the problems of</u>
13. <u>literacy among three students of widely differing</u>
14. <u>cultures.</u> . . . This is not nearly so general as it
15. sounds . . . <u>First of all, what is literacy? Is there a</u>
16. <u>widely accepted standard?</u> . . . Let's take a look at the
17. card again. . . . hmm . . . Am I jumping into this a little too
18. quickly? . . . "First of all, what is literacy?" . . . Maybe I
19. don't need to keep asking questions . . . uh . . . <u>The</u>
20. <u>requirements of the country in an economic, social,</u>
21. <u>political sense seem to be the</u> . . . uh . . . <u>determining</u> . . . I
22. don't want to put myself into a corner here . . . "seems to
23. be the determining" <u>factors in deciding literacy.</u> . . . If
24. I'm going to say that it might be wise to explain what I
25. mean with an example . . . hmmm . . . and I don't want to
26. contradict myself later on . . . So . . . "The
27. requirements of the country" . . . the political, economic,
28. etc., requirements "seem to be the determining factors in
29. deciding" <u>legal</u> "literacy." . . . Well, in brackets, (<u>In</u>
30. <u>Barbardos, for instance, the government quotes a figure</u>
31. <u>of 98% literacy.</u> . . . Uh, ok, I've already said that's a
32. legal definition . . . <u>This means that 98% of the adult</u>
33. <u>males in the country can sign their name on a marriage</u>
34. <u>register.)</u> [indent] <u>On the other hand</u> . . . OK, I'm still
35. asking the question what is literacy . . . "On the other
36. hand" <u>a literary tradition heavily influences</u> . . . hmmm
37. . . . <u>the reading and writing skills of a population.</u> . . .
38. Another . . . hmmm . . . Well, we've still got to define
39. literacy. It's true that a literary tradition heavily

40. influences that but we haven't said what it is and we
41. can't use that tradition to make a definition ... uh ...
42. But what we want to say is that A functioning literacy
43. seems to depend only partially ... let's ask the question
44. (if at all) ... hmmm ... "only partially"· on on the
45. actual ... rests ... uh huh ... on the actual social
46. requirements ... uh, so we can't really ... uh ... Let's
47. see. What's the point of that? I want to say that
48. legal definitions of literacy are inadequate but that's
49. a negative statement. I need something positive. ...

This writer is in the act of producing a typical literate essay, in which he is attempting to lay out a relatively explicit, autonomous, reasoned exposition about a situation in the objective world. But it is important to note how the words in this evolving text function for the writer—what they mean within the context of his work. Consider the sentence: "But is this a localized observation or does the same situation arise elsewhere?" (ll. 6–7). This statement (or question) might appear, on the face of it, message-focused, detached from the writer, referring to an objective reality, a "situation elsewhere" which, if not existing in fact, certainly exists in the text world under creation. This sentence gestures to some world of literacy problems. But consider the pragmatic, or "current" meaning that the sentence has for the writer: it is there for him to "get an immediate handle on things" (ll. 8–9). That is what the sentence really means. The writer had to bring this sentence into his context to open up some public space in which to keep going. Its meaning relates to the act of writing in progress (the situation right here) as much as to a situation elsewhere.

Of course, this sentence allows the writer to get a handle on things in part because of what he knows is going on at the reader's end. Scanning his text, the writer becomes aware of how, inadvertently, he may be implying a discourse topic (literacy in the United States) that he does not want to imply. He needs to change the subject fast. So, while he turns the topic to other cultures as sites of literacy problems, he also conveys a metacommunicative message ("See, I'm not talking about U.S. literacy after all. Don't get too invested in that.") This writer understands that readers read for current meaning too. They occupy the same public context as the writer and read not only for what a text is "about" in terms of message but how it is about what the writer and reader are doing.

Readers read for what a text is saying about the mutual situation right here.

This excerpt also demonstrates how constantly the writer scans his text as a way to monitor the intersubjective context, to establish or reconfirm "what's going on" or "where things stand now" in the public situation. Phrases like, "Uh, ok, I've already said that's a legal definition" (ll. 31–32) or "OK, I'm still asking the question what is literacy" (ll. 34–35) show the writer keeping himself oriented to what is in current shared focus as guidance for proceeding. That same kind of intersubjective monitoring (What is this language saying about what I am doing and need to be doing?) allows him to detect what *is not* in current shared focus but may need to be: "If I'm going to say that it might be wise to explain what I mean with an example" (ll. 23–25). At some points the writer even seems to talk directly to a reader, for instance, when he urges patience and indulgence in the observation that "This is not nearly so general as it sounds" (ll. 14–15). What is demonstrated by this protocol is that all levels of decision-making in composing, from planning (add example) to word choice (no need to repeat *legal*) take place within a sense of the here-and-now public conditions that writer and reader can lay claim to together. While Flower and Hayes stress how plans generate text, we must also stress how texts generate plans.

In the strong-text view, written language, particularly exposition, has been considered message-focused, impersonal, autonomous. The interpersonal channel is said to be submerged in favor of "ideation" as Halliday calls it, and texts are said to refer mostly inward to themselves. That is how the insular text world (the world of words) is created. But approaching written language from the perspectives of writers and readers in the act casts literate language in a decidedly different light. "Reference" for the writer and reader at work must always include reference to "things right here," that is, "things as they stand so far for me and you." Reference in written texts is always to the practical actions and accomplishments of writing and reading and is thus intensely contextualized and intersubjective.

This is especially important to stress in relation to the logic of written argumentation. In strong-text formulations, material inscription is said to lift out logic for conscious, separate reflection. But consider the logical fuddle this writer contends with in the latter part of the protocol (ll. 37–46). He certainly works from an implicit sense of the requirements of academic exposition, concerned as he is with the ideals of accuracy and truth and care with evidence and definition of terms. Yet this thinking through of definition, argument, and the logical progression of argument proceeds within the constraints of the intersubjective situation ("we haven't said what it is" [ll. 39–40]), the effort to change that situation to make room for the argument ("let's ask the question" [l. 43]), and the realization of new constraints created by that language ("so we can't really, uh, let's see" [ll. 46–47]). I do not wish to deny or minimize the enabling power of writing to sustain and augment logical reflection. I am suggesting, however, that logical accomplishments occur within the pressure of intersubjective awareness. What this writer is reflecting on primarily are the means by which he and his reader *together* can reach his point, that is, the intersubjective conditions that must exist for both of them finally to "get it."

A similar process occurs in the following excerpt by the same writer, where again the written text accentuates for him not so much the means by which argument is structured as the means by which an intersubjective situation accomplishes argument or enables it to proceed. In the excerpt the writer has just completed a nonstop drafting of one whole paragraph of an essay based on "inventories" that the class had done of all the writing that they kept in their domiciles. The aim of the assignment was to consider what the inventories said about how writing was serving students in their daily lives, and then to consider how valid the inventories were as a guide for answering that question. The writer thought the inventories were not very reliable at all. As the episode begins, he stops writing, pauses, then begins to scan, asking himself, in effect, "Where are we?" or "Where do we go from here?"

> hmmm . . . So what we've done so far is to analyze the inventory itself, determine its significance as far as the role of writing is concerned in a student's life or in students' lives in general. . . . uh . . . I think I've shown that there's a great deal of individual interpretation involved. . . . I'm now trying to talk about the general characteristics of an inventory. . . . Yes, I think we've more or less condensed what we've said before except that we haven't talked about literacy yet. . . . Most of the arguments against a literacy study have been hinted at already so are we undercutting ourselves? . . . The common factors of literacy, the relationship we've got, what appears to be a valid relationship. . . . Now the literacy study depends upon assumptions. . . . We've already shown what those assumptions are. . . . It's all circumstantial. . . .

It might be said that this writer is checking the text to see how well it is realizing his organizational plan or that he is using the text to refresh his memory of the plan. But in this scanning, the writer is really testing the intersubjective atmosphere, sizing up the extent to which the public grounds will allow the next move he wants to make and the extent to which a reader might already be sharing the key perspective that his argument hinges on ("it's all circumstantial"). The writer's concern here is not with the validity or coherence of his argument but with what a reader is making of the argument and whether that now provides him with an opportunity to keep going.

Let us consider again the profiles of expert and novice writers that emerge in process-oriented research. Experts spend a considerable amount of their composing time and effort in building, maintaining, and attending to a working context, a complex and dynamic sense of "where things stand now" that helps them formulate, modify, and realize plans and goals. This context sustains not merely the semantic meaning of a developing text but a wider meaning for the composing act itself. The developing text is a product of this context, but it is also an important constituent of it, as it accomplishes further and further the shared public grounds from which a writer keeps going. Certainly the behind-the-scenes accomplishments of literate acts compels a rethinking of writing and reading as "decontextualized" language skills. While writers and readers do have to proceed independently of a shared real time and space, it is inaccurate to characterize this process as decontextualized in any sense for, if anything, separation of writer and reader intensifies attention to the ways intersubjective context works to accomplish meaning. The making of social context—which is required in all language exchanges, oral or written—becomes an overriding and conscious consideration in writing and reading.

The developing text plays a central role in making and maintaining context (for writer as much as for reader), but this is not the same thing as saying that writing and reading rely on semantic context (how words relate to surrounding words) for interpretation. Because writers and readers do not merely have to keep a message going but also have to keep a whole process going, they have to understand how textual language refers to what they are in the act of doing—how it refers to the processes of writing and reading that are under way. That is why attention to the state of context (one's own and the reader's) permeates the oral protocols of expert writers.

This awareness tends to be absent or ineffectively realized in the processes of novice writers, who spend most of their time and effort attending to the text as product. They focus a majority of their planning time on "what to say next" and are frequently preoccupied with surface correctness. The processes of novice or ineffective writers are often unsystematic and fraught with frustrating and unproductive formulas (what Mike Rose calls "rigid rules and inflexible plans") that they impose generically on every writing task. Novice writers frequently appear less audience-aware than experts or unable to translate that awareness into strategies for themselves or their texts. Novice writers also tend to monitor and reflect upon their processes much less often than experts. As a result, novices' sense of "what is going on here" tends to be quite general, static, and flat, not changing much from the beginning of a writing episode to the end. Novices quite literally do not know *how* to write in that they do not know how to carry on the work of writing nor accomplish sense through it. In keeping with the developing argument of this chapter, we can say that novice writers do not have access to the metacommunicative meaning of written language that experts see and exploit readily.

Consider, for instance, the following excerpt from a think-aloud protocol of an eighteen-year-old college freshman, a Korean-American, middle-class male who was enrolled in the same introductory composition class as our earlier writer. Though obviously far from illiterate, this writer had tremendous difficulty composing essays for the course, spending hour upon frustrated hour producing short, sketchy papers that he was most unsatisfied with. Further, although this writer could read college-level material with comprehension, he could not easily separate main ideas from subordinating ones in order to prepare written summaries. He also matched the profile of the novice writer in that he concentrated a great deal on surface correctness and revised very little from draft to draft.

In this excerpt the writer, like the earlier representative, is at work on an argumentative essay about the alleged literacy crisis among American high-school students. In a precomposing interview he had expressed confidence in completing the assignment because he said he had prepared a similar argument the previous year for presentation on his high-school debate team. His essay attempts to argue that critics of American education fail to consider its democratic mission to educate everyone, not just the privileged few. We join him at a point where he, like the first writer, decides he must define "literacy." (I have underlined the

words he is writing down and placed in quotation marks the passages
that he is reading or rereading from his own text.)

1. Then, let's see . . . define literacy . . . literacy . . . Gotta
2. look it up in the dictionary now . . . okay, literacy . . .
3. Then we present the dictionary definition. . . . Literacy.
4. It's a <u>Noun,</u> and it's <u>The ability to read and write.</u>
5. Simple as that, the ability to read and write. <u>That's</u>
6. <u>taken from the American Heritage Dictionary</u> . . . I didn't
7. get that handout . . . the American Heritage Dictionary <u>of</u>
8. <u>the English Language.</u> . . . Well, I can do this later. Just
9. get the basic ideas down right now, that's all I want
10. to do and worry about that later. . . . "Are we producing a
11. a generation of illiterates? Many people perceive that
12. there is an illiteracy crisis; however, they take a
13. narrow view of things. Literacy. Noun. The ability
14. to read and write. That's from the the American
15. Heritage Dictionary . . . okay, um, the English Language."
16. . . . <u>First,</u> comma <u>who determines</u> determines illiteracy . . .
17. determines <u>literacy?</u> . . . Let's put it that way . . . um . . .
18. "determines literacy" . . . "Literacy. The ability to read
19. and write." . . . Let's look over my ideas. I ask the
20. question. Does it reflect consideration of the audience?
21. Is my organizing idea there and building a relationship?
22. Now I want to say produce the basic belief . . . [proceeds
23. to read the entire draft so far] . . . "This definition"
24. strike this . . . "This definition taken from the American
25. Heritage Dictionary" . . . "Heritage Dictionary of the
26. English Language" . . . "taken from the American Heritage
27. Dictionary" <u>is</u> an is <u>a straightforward</u> . . . that's what it
28. is . . . straightforward <u>definition</u> . . . "This definition
29. taken from the American Heritage Dictionary of the
30. English Language is straightforward" . . . don't be too
31. verbose . . . "straightforward" period . . . It does not set
32. guidelines. . . . What word do I want to use? . . . <u>It does</u>
33. <u>not set up a scale to determine what literacy is.</u> . . .
34. period . . . I should have brought my thesaurus. . . . "It does
35. not set up a scale to determine what literacy is." <u>It</u>
36. <u>states that it is the ability</u> . . . underline ability . . . <u>to</u>

37. read and write. It does not say read and write
38. proficiently or coherently or anything else. . . . period . . .
39. I have discovered that society has added those
40. adverbs . . . those are adverbs, no? . . . "I have discovered
41. that society has added those adverbs" to the
42. definition. . . . oh blank . . . "It does not say read and
43. write proficiently or coherently or anything else. I
44. have discovered that society has added those adverbs
45. to the definition." . . . period . . . Am I getting somewhere?
46. Let me think. . . . Yeah, I'm getting somewhere. I'm
47. showing that society . . . "the definition taken from the
48. American Heritage Dictionary of the English Language is
49. straightforward. It does not set up a scale to
50. determine what literacy is. It states that it is the
51. ability to read and write. It does not say that it is
52. the ability to read and write proficiently or coherently
53. or anything else. I have discovered that society has
54. added those adverbs to the definition." . . . period . . . This
55. adds . . . Since those adverbs have been placed onto the
56. definition . . . No, what's the word I want to use? . . . added
57. to "the definition" . . . "Since these adverbs have been
58. added to the definition" . . . "added to the definition"
59. . . . "the definition" . . .

To put this episode in strong-text terms, this writer attends to the literal words of his text to the almost total exclusion of everything else. In fact, reading and rereading his text was virtually the only strategy he had for planning and revising (save for regular consultations with a pocket dictionary, thesaurus, and Bartlett's *Familiar Quotations*).[9] He gives very little conscious attention to maintaining a working context as a source for meaning or helpful orientation, nor does he seem to take the text as more than an object to be tinkered with or to be used as a kind of incantatory chant from which, with luck, the next word or phrase will spring. The writer does pause on occasion in an effort to glean a wider sense of "where things stand now." This occurs at lines 19–21 and 45–47. But the first pause seems to be a pro forma bow to some concepts and advice that had been stressed in his textbook. The writer does not seem to particularize *how* his text reflects a consideration of audience nor *what* his organizing idea and its relationships are. Instead, he becomes distracted by the text before him, an event that recurs at his next attempt to assess (ll. 45–47).

Despite this writer's tendency to go "blank," his protocols were not entirely bereft of attention to intersubjective context. In the following excerpt, which had come very early in his drafting of the argumentative essay on the literacy crisis, he stops drafting and begins to scan his text, considering how he is appealing to his audience:

> Well, I appeal, I try and appeal to the American way of education being available to anyone no matter his race, religion, sex, color, or creed, and yet I show that people overlook this benefit and then they find something wrong . . . and so then I pose the question about the education system failing and they think it is and they think about the situation and I guess I would be appealing to families generally or people in school. . . . [reads] . . . "Is our education system failing?" . . . They reflect on that. . . . [reads again] . . . "Are we producing a generation of illiterates?" . . . and then they reflect on that too. . . . um . . . [He begins to read the text from the top.]

The writer demonstrates here a more particular conception of his readers ("families generally or people in school") and, especially, a more particular sense of how his text is embodying that conception. In other words, he shows a fundamental awareness that his text is being read: he envisions a reader responding to his text and the relevance that response has for what he is doing. But one of his difficulties throughout all of his recorded writing sessions was his inability to convert this general awareness into a decision about what to do next. In the episode above, for instance, he is unable to ask himself what might be entailed in the reflections he is ascribing to his readers and, more pertinent, what that might mean for the development of his text.

When Writers Read: Maintaining a Context of Involvement

In examining the contrasts in the writing processes of these two writers, it became obvious that the difference lay in the expert's ability to muster and manage context, both a private "working" context and a public, intersubjectively accomplished context, both of which provided guidance for what to do next. It also became clear that the expert writer used his own developing text as a way of maintaining that context. Although the novice was clearly focused on his emerging text and often read and reread his developing draft, he did not read it in the kind of double way that the expert did, for its communicative *and* metacommunicative messages.

As many researchers have observed, pausing to read or scan one's text is a ubiquitous activity in writing, occurring throughout drafting and revising. Several empirical studies, notably by Bridwell, Perl, and Pianko, have focused on writers' reading or scanning as a way to evaluate how well a text realizes an intention or as a way to edit for error or mistranscription. Margaret Atwell found that reading during writing enabled writers to adhere to global text plans. In an extremely interesting formulation, Nancy Shanklin has suggested that a writer, like Louise Rosenblatt's reader, enters into a "transactional" relationship with the developing text. During the process of writing, a writer's evolving text activates relevant schemas in the writer's mind that then promote further writing. (See also a recent article by Keith Grant-Davie for a useful overview.)

Reading during writing becomes especially intriguing for an investigation of the role of intersubjectivity in literate experience. Stopping to read a developing text is a tangible moment in which a writer attends to the public context—a moment for seeing where things stand now. However, this is not exactly how researchers—especially Flower and Hayes—have typically characterized the role of reading. In fact, in Flower and Hayes' current "cognitive process" model, reading per se is subsumed under the more generic process of what they call reviewing. According to Flower and Hayes writers read what they have written "either as a springboard to further translating or with an eye to systematically evaluating and/or revising their text" ("Cognitive Process Theory" 374).

Interestingly, an earlier version of the Hayes and Flower model divided the process of reviewing into "reading" and "editing" ("Identifying" 11). Later, perhaps in part to distinguish more clearly between text-making and underlying cognition, the terms were changed to "evaluating" and "revising." Removing "reading" from the model was an unfortunate change in terminology, for a couple of reasons. First, reading is a distinctive phenomenon in the composing process. It occurs like translating (which is Flower and Hayes' term for writing down) as a major boundary, marking a likely place for a writer's current mental representation to undergo significant change. Second, the shift in termi-nology falsely narrows the primary function of reading to evaluating (checking to see if a text is adequately realizing a writer's plan or whether it is "OK" to keep writing). But, as the oral protocols, especially of the expert writer, revealed, reading plays a more fundamentally generative role than that.[10] The language of a developing text is con-stantly pushing open a writer's horizon of possiblities at the same time it is accomplishing a public history that the writer is accountable for. The developing text permeates every aspect of composing with its mean-ing. The act of going public stimulates the cycles of goal-setting, planning, drafting, and so on that form the "dynamic" of composing.

Flower and Hayes treat the public text as a kind of end-of-the-line result—the repository of a writer's solutions. What I am suggesting is the text is better seen as a writer's emerging problem, as it delineates the unfolding social reality through which a writer must continue to try to be understood and in which a writer's decisions (including plans) are taking place. Reading is the means by which effective writers stay oriented to intersubjective reality—the way they stay involved with what is going on in public. Reading is a writer's prime source of metacommun-icative meaning, a prime guide for what to do now. The differences in the profiles between expert and novice writers begin with how they read their unfolding texts. Expert writers see metacommunicative mean-ing that less skilled writers do not see.

Let us now consider patterns of reading during writing by the two writers under discussion, Mark (the expert) and Paul (the novice). What I want to point out are sharp differences in the uses that the two writers made of their emerging texts and how metacommunicative reading, especially by Mark, helped to sustain the social and cognitive contexts of composing.

The following descriptive data is drawn from a larger study of some twenty-five hours of think-aloud protocols rendered by the two students. Here I concentrate on three think-aloud protocols by each student as he wrote first drafts on three assigned topics.[11] Both writers knew they would have an opportunity to revise the drafts before they were formally due in their composition class. My questions were these: What role did reading play in the conduct of the two writers' composing processes? What were the writers doing immediately before and immediately after reading occurred? What differences emerge between the writers in their uses of reading during writing? I counted "reading" as any instance in which a writer interrupted other composing activities to read or scan a sentence or more of inscription. The results reported here are based on 139 "readings," 57 by Mark and 82 by Paul.

Once drafting began, both writers devoted about one-fourth of their composing time to reading. And reading was associated for both writers with a wide range of composing activities, including planning (all mental acts of generating ideas, organizing, and goal setting); writing (all instances of initial inscribing); assessing (acts of evaluating inscribed text); revising and editing (all changes in inscribed text);[12] orienting (an act that lies somewhere between planning and assessing in which a writer essentially asks "where are we now?"); and resuming (starting up again after random interruptions). But as the statistics in Table 1 reveal, the two writers differed markedly in the way they integrated reading with other composing activities.

Table 1

Activities Occurring Immediately Prior to and After Reading by Writer

	Prior to Reading		After Reading	
Planning				
	Mark:	21%	Mark:	23%
	Paul:	40%	Paul:	15%
Writing				
	Mark:	45%	Mark:	25%
	Paul:	44%	Paul:	49%
Assessing				
	Mark:	24.5%	Mark:	19%
	Paul:	4%	Paul:	19%
Revising/Editing				
	Mark:	3.5%	Mark:	25%
	Paul:	.01%	Paul:	15%
Orienting				
	Mark:	—	Mark:	9%
	Paul:	—	Paul:	2%
Resuming				
	Mark:	5%	Mark:	—
	Paul:	12%	Paul:	—

These statistics paint a familiar study in contrast between expert and nonexpert writers. Paul relied almost totally on a plan-read-write or write-read-assess pattern in his composing, with reading serving primarily to help to plan the next sentence or as a means to render a (usually negative) assessment of what he had just written down. For Mark, on the other hand, reading was much more knitted into the performance and management of the whole writing act. He was doing more varied things in conjunction with reading. For Paul, planning typically induced reading and reading induced assessment, whereas for Mark, reading often induced planning and assessment induced reading. Mark also was four times more likely than Paul to use his text to orient himself before proceeding. Flower and Hayes report that expert writers work from mental representations that are both more dynamic and more particular than those of less skilled writers. The way that Mark invoked reading in a rich interplay among planning, drafting, assessing, revising, and orienting reveals the role of reading in maintaining that dynamic, particular representation. Although both writers read their texts with about the same frequency, the uses they made of that reading differed considerably. We might say these are differences between text-making and context-making: Paul concentrated on producing a literal text while Mark distributed his attention more widely in maintaining (and exploiting) his situation-at-hand.

This difference becomes even starker with the addition of two more sets of statistics. First is a breakdown (Table 2) of the kinds of planning that were associated with each writer's reading. That is, I looked at all instances of planning that preceded or followed reading and placed them in Flower and Hayes' categories of "to do" plans (ex., "I think I'm going to approach this from the point of view of an observer"); "to say" plans (ex., "I want to take a stab at what the major role of writing is in general"); and "process" plans (ex., "I'm going to underline that because I may need to come back to that later"). The outcome corroborates a familiar pattern in expert-novice studies in which expert writers attend constantly to pragmatic planning while novice writers focus mostly on what to say next.

Earlier I noted that literate orientation requires knowing how to read a text for what it is telling you about what you need to be doing. Here we find dramatic evidence of Mark's ability to read in that way, as some 70 percent of his planning around reading is given to high-level rhetorical designing and managing of the writing act itself. For Paul, things are just the reverse. Nearly 70 percent of his plans around reading focus on literal textual content—another example of how message-focus and text-centeredness lead away from (not toward) literate orientation. This contrast (the "70 percent factor") is quite similar to an expert-

Table 2
Types of Planning Surrounding Reading by Writer

"To do" planning	Mark:	52%	Paul:	23%
"To say" planning	Mark:	28%	Paul:	69%
"Process" planning	Mark:	20%	Paul:	8%

Total number of planning episodes involving reading: Mark = 25; Paul = 46.

novice study by Flower and Hayes in which they found experienced writers "generated up to 60 per cent of their new ideas in response to the larger rhetorical problem" . . . [while for poor writers] 70 per cent of their new ideas were statements about the topic alone without concern for the larger rhetorical problem" ("Cognition of Discovery" 30). Looking at the role of reading in generating and sustaining "ideas" deepens the understanding of the social origins of expert-novice differences. It also sheds light on how the reading side of one's literate ability relates to the writing side. Whereas Flower and Hayes might say that in our study Mark was solving a different problem than Paul, we could just as profitably say that Mark was reading his text in a much different way from Paul. Mark read for metacommunicative meaning.

A second telling statistic rounds out the story of the role of the evolving text in propelling composing. I recorded the number of times each writer read more than one sentence and the number of times each scanned his text. In scanning, writers backed up (usually across two or more paragraphs) and paraphrased the text, summing up the current state of affairs. Mark scanned his text twice as often as Paul. Forty percent of Mark's 57 readings involved scanning or reading more than one sentence. For Paul, this portion was only 25 percent of his 82 readings. Further, for Mark, scanning was highly associated with orienting and assessing.

I suggested earlier that the evolving text exerts a powerful influence on the whole of the composing process to the extent to which it delineates the public context through which a writer must continue to try to share understandings. To write down words is to give them over to a public sphere where their meaning or potential meaning is somehow always bigger, and more demanding, than private sense. To write is to deliver words into the domain of the we. Rolf Kjolseth describes the grounds of the "we" in language comprehension in terms of what "we" know is specifically relevant here and now. He writes: "a 'we' knows this knowledge and can lay claims to it, and sanction its relevance. 'We' are its witnesses and representatives. And thus our 'weness' is sedimented in this emergent knowledge and each use of the emergent ground exemplifies this 'we' " (65).

Composing entails a constant combing of this domain for it represents what Rommetveit calls "the temporarily shared social reality" that writer and reader are establishing together. And, as I have been suggesting, reading is the primary means by which writers maintain involvement with this evolving social reality.

A final example from Mark's third protocol demonstrates, in its intensity and complexity, the dynamic intersubjective play that infuses the cognition of writing and the powerful shaping role of the public text on the whole of a writing act. Mark is writing about an interview that he has conducted with a French-born poet and professor of comparative literature. The aim of the interview assignment, in part, was to talk to someone outside of class about writing and about any of the issues that the class had been exploring together. Mark had decided to talk to the poet (Professor S.) about new technologies in communication as well as the alleged literacy crisis among American students. The episode begins with Mark reading over a couple of sentences that he had just drafted. (The words that Mark subsequently writes down are underlined.)

> [Reading] "I smiled and nodded agreement, wondering at the same time if the professor had not made a few assumptions that might be characteristic of a writer or a non-scientist in regard to the machine. Of course there was supposed to be an antipathy between the artist and the machine." . . . And I can't use machine twice but I'm leaving it for now. . . . "I thought of Descartes and wondered."
> . . . [stops reading] . . . Oh, the idea of going off on a tangent is attractive but . . . hmm . . . so why? Where were the assumptions made? . . . [reads again] . . . "With a cautious smile he assured me that the creative process itself could not for him be replaced by the machine." . . . all right . . . "The writer must conduct the creative part of the process on his own, he felt." . . . all right . . . Let's uh let's continue. I'm rather tied to the actual structure of the interview. . . . hmmm . . . <u>Professor S was convinced of the reality of the 'crisis'</u> . . . and now this is a this is a break from the rest of the interview and it's obvious that I ask a sort of current topic question . . . <u>in literacy among U.S. students, as I had expected</u>

before I asked the ... No, I can't can't use <u>current question</u> because of its double meaning. So I ask I ask I as I had expected before I asked the <u>topic</u> question. ... It's really at that point more or less working to a scheme. ... Well, let's sort of narrate the rest of this. ... It's really a narrative but we'll do something about that later. ...

This episode demonstrates the kind of intricate conversation that goes on between writer and public text as the writer monitors the shareable reality in which he is working and the various strata of meanings that the text represents. After rejecting the opportunity that the text offers him for going off on a tangent, Mark reenters the text essentially to assess "what is going on here." He reads the text for its current public status, a move that provokes the inevitable question: What assumptions does the text refer to? Rereading the text from a more consciously public perspective, he determines the assumptions have, in fact, been sufficiently implied and thus require no more elaboration. The next sequence is an exquisite example of intersubjective monitoring as Mark shifts from the implications of his text to the inferences of the reader ("it's obvious that I ask a sort of current topic question"). Then he becomes caught in the ambiguity among the contextual, private, and textual meanings of "current"—the "current event" connotation that the literacy crisis carries, the "current" question in the original interview sequence that Mark worrisomely feels tied to, and the "current" question that the reader would be happening onto in the public "current" of the evolving text. In this episode we see what makes writing such a dynamic cognitive experience, as going public with language involves a constant upsetting, deepening, and discovering of meaning.

Conclusion: Literacy from a Process Perspective

As Chapter One demonstrated, the central tenet of strong-text theories of literacy is that to understand acts of reading and writing we must understand the circumstances and technology of textuality. My argument is just the reverse: to understand textuality we must understand the acts of writing and reading. In shifting the perspective from product to process, most of the strong-text characterizations of literacy appear unsatisfactory.

Above all, the text as artifact is not at the center of consideration in acts of fluent writing and reading. Rather, the focus of interpretation is on the broader accomplishment of the act itself. "Meaning" in written discourse is primarily a matter of finding and maintaining the means by which what you are doing (as writer or reader) can keep making sense. In strong-text accounts, literacy is described as the way of the text and the literate orientation appears as a textlike orientation. But, in fact, it is the least successful writers and readers who perceive the literate enterprise as a matter of literal text-making or text-taking.

A focus on literacy-in-action draws attention to the context-making processes that underlie writing and reading. In strong-text accounts, literacy is affiliated with a decontextualization of language and an ability to divorce oneself from contexts of action to operate on or through the fixed semantic conventions of autonomous text. From a process perspective, writers and readers (especially expert ones) work hard to develop and stay oriented to a particular, here-and-now, action-centered context, and they know how to use every scrap of that context in guiding meaning. The overriding difference that emerges in studies of expert and novice writers and readers lies in this ability to accomplish and maintain the broad contextual conditions that allow a writer or a reader to decide "what to do now."

In strong-text accounts, becoming literate is said to require coming to understand how different literacy is from orality. Especially, according to David Olson, it requires the ability to untangle language from people, to learn that written language can be meaningful independent from human actions. But a process perspective suggests something else. Learning to read and write is learning about the actions of reading and writing and how written discourse relates to those actions. Literate language, like oral language, comes embedded in the practical, pragmatic contexts of action that constitute writing and reading. Becoming literate requires gaining an understanding of these contexts of action.

In the strong-text view, the separate material text is said to embody anonymous knowledge, knowledge without knowers, and to shine back at people their own abstraction, anonymity, and separateness. Texts are characterized as walls against which to project private thought. But to see how texts function for writers and readers in-the-act is to arrive at a much different characterization. Texts shine back at writers and readers a developing allegiance to a common orientation, a specific and intimate present that each relies upon for meaning and order, a common knowledge accomplished uniquely by "the we," writer and reader, whose paths through the text grow difficult to distinguish from one another. In the strong-text view, meaning is arbitrated out of abstract conventions, such as generic structures and dictionary definitions. But as the protocol of Mark wrestling with the "current topic" demonstrated so well, written meaning is conferred from the idiosyncratic configuration of things-so-far, the are-you-with-me, oh-yeah-right, let's-give-it-a-go accomplishments of writing and reading.

The next two chapters will continue to mount a challenge to strong-text theories of literacy by turning more specifically to the language of public texts. Understanding how acts of writing and reading are constituted by intersubjective contexts opens the way to seeing material texts in a new light: as documents that essentially refer to the acts of writing and reading in progress. Written texts talk about what the writers and readers of them are doing. This metacommunicative view of written discourse is at odds with prevailing conceptions. As we have seen, in the strong-text view, when common time, space, and setting are eliminated in the move from the oral to the literate, writer and reader are free (or compelled) to concentrate more on pure propositional content. This shift, in the strong-text view, gives expository texts the qualities of message-focus, self-referentiality, and autonomy. Typical expository texts are said to make explicit the background knowledge that is needed for their comprehension. The following chapters invite a different interpretation, suggesting that when time, space, and setting drop out, metacommunication becomes the only game in town. What written texts make explicit are the processes by which understanding is getting accomplished. And that is what you have to understand in order to understand texts.

Chapter Three

The Language of Involvement

In an essay called "What Happens to Bodies if Genes Act for Themselves?" Stephen J. Gould reviews and then rejects various evolutionary arguments for why certain DNA duplicates itself tens to hundreds of times. Gould concludes that duplication happens for no better reason than that a body does not mind it. He then observes:

> I can almost hear the disappointment and anger of some readers: "That bastard Gould. He led us along for pages, and now he gives an explanation that is no explanation at all. It just plain happens, and that's all there is to it. Is this a joke or a counsel of despair?" I beg to differ from this not entirely hypothetic adversary (a composite constructed from several real responses I have received to verbal descriptions of the selfish DNA hypothesis). This explanation seems hokey only in the context of adherence to traditional views that all important features must be adaptations and that bodies are *the* agent of Darwinian processes. The radical content of selfish DNA is not the explanation itself, but the reformulated perspective that must be assimilated before the explanation confers any satisfaction. (172)

Gould goes on to show that DNA is like other creatures of nature: it will reproduce itself in the absence of contraception. But it is the author's outburst of direct address that stands interesting. The passage could be called an example of unbridled audience awareness, a place where writer drops dissemblance and takes on directly the imagined reaction of a skeptic. Deborah Tannen almost certainly would classify it as "involvement-focused," and William Vande Kopple ("Some Exploratory Discourse") would call it "metadiscourse," discourse about the discourse.

The passage is interesting for exposing the kinds of musings and mutterings that writers and readers frequently address to each other subtextually, as think-aloud protocols particularly have demonstrated.[1] But here Gould brings the subtext into sudden and radical view and, in doing so, brings to a stop (at least for a moment) the performance in progress. He reveals the condition of the writer's interpretive grounds, which normally remain below the threshhold of direct reference. He exposes the writer's gauge of the reader not merely in the rhetorical sense of anticipating a different opinion but in the sense of acknowledging what a reader—his reader—has been doing for the past couple of pages. Gould is writing directly about what has been going on at the other end.

Gould's outburst is not, of course, without rhetorical design and effect: disarming readers by exaggeration, calling himself a name only for the opportunity to dazzle those who have not kept up with his drift. He is, the passage reminds us, a clever fellow. But, as a piece of metadiscourse, the passage primarily refers to the act of reading and how it is protruding upon the act of writing. It is about how the reader-in-the-act is functioning as part of Gould's interpretive grounds and the way Gould believes the reader must see the state of affairs in order for the discourse to remain viable. Gould can hear readers summing up what has just transpired ("it just plain happens") and labeling it "a joke" or "a counsel of despair." But if readers have reached that conclusion, it is because they are applying inappropriate assumptions. Hokey is in the eye of the beholder. Gould's passage says, in essence, "If you have found my explanation a joke, you are reading it in the wrong way. Here is how you have to read it instead." The last sentence of the passage is not about DNA and not even about Gould's argument; rather is is about how the argument has to be (re)read: "The radical content of selfish DNA is not the explanation itself, but the reformulated perspective that must be assimilated before the explanation confers any satisfaction." These are explicit directions for how to read the text, how to "take" its various aspects.

Gould's reference to the act of reading (and writing) his text may be unusual for being so direct and extended. But, actually, writing of all kinds is filled with overt and covert allusions to the cognitive presence of writer and reader, what I shall call repeatedly the "we" of the discourse. Although this presence must remain "hypothetic" on both ends, the dynamic involvement with the other shapes and propels writing and reading. And evidence of this involvement is all over the place in written discourse.

My aim in this chapter is to trace various forms of the language of involvement as it appears in written texts. The examination not only will point up direct references to the acts of writing and reading but also will consider some of the bread and butter features of written language, particularly cohesion and lexical explicitness, as aspects and indicators of involvement. On the basis of this textual analysis, we will be able to reapproach literacy and involvement from what I hope will be a fuller and more satisfying perspective.

A Functional Reinterpretation of Text

Strong text, as described in Chapter One, is strong by virtue of losing indexicality and achieving self-referentiality. The alphabet, released from reliance on crude semblance to the actual world, provides the necessary elements of arbitrariness and opacity (Frawley 26). Genre formulas, cohesion, integrated syntax, and other marks of textualness complete the revolution into autonomy by providing the means by which texts can refer mainly to themselves and to each other. Written discourse abides in the text world, where social relationships give way to semantic ones and meaning is made deductively, in the private mind, out of the conventional material surfaces of language-on-its-own. This great semiotic escape of writing from social, temporal strictures is, in the strong-text view, what makes literate orientation an antisocial orientation: an ability to follow written language into its own dimension, separated from people. Literate exchange is always indirect exchange, according to strong-text accounts. The arbitrariness of written language makes it an abstractly arbitrated language. Literate connections must be negotiated not out of particular experience with the other but out of prolonged formal education in which we cultivate knowledge of language conventions and existing text worlds.

But the nature of texts and literate orientation can be imagined another way. Here, the social relationship of writer and reader, rather than being in subordination or atrophy during textual exchange, takes central focus as a main problem of consciousness. What rises to the surface in the literate orientation and is carried in the history of texts are the means by which people maintain the processes of intersubjective life. As the literate is normally contrasted with the oral, real-world orientations of time, place, setting, and participants drop out of relative concern on the literate side: literate language is free to concentrate on pure, explicit propositional content. Full-blown expository prose originates and models a fully stipulated world of statements. Here I suggest an opposite move in the development of literacy. When the real world drops out, literate language concentrates on the means that keep human intersubjectivity going. The participants and what they are doing become all important in literate exchange because that is all the exchange has to go on. To put this in the framework of indexicality, written language may no longer gesture out to the material world right here, but it does retain indexicality, gesturing always out of the text to the underlying human acts of writing and reading in progress. Contrary to prevailing characterizations, then, written discourse is radically metacommunicative and thereby radically social. What is always being made explicit in written discourse is how understanding is being reached.

What, then, are the resources of written text that maintain metacommunication, those resources that function to index the acts of writing and reading?

Messages of involvement. A large body of scholarship already exists on the social dynamics of texts. Most of this research has to do with (1) metadiscourse and (2) communicative dynamism, as it is manifested in such relationships as given-new and theme-rheme (referring to a two-part structure of a sentence, the first securing a focus and the second elaborating upon that focus).[2] Metadiscourse refers to aspects of text that are about the discourse itself. Metadiscourse does not expand the propositional content of texts, as William Vande Kopple has explained it, but rather explicitly calls attention to the processes of communication that are under way ("Some Exploratory Discourse" 85). Rather than make claims about states of affairs in the world, metadiscourse instead refers to the status of the textual communication. Vande Kopple provides a catalogue of metadiscourse features, ranging from text connectors (*first, next*); reminders of material presented earlier in a text; announcements of upcoming materials; topicalizers (*for example*); code glosses (parenthetical expressions, definitions); illocution markers (*I will argue*); validity markers (*perhaps*); narrators(*according to*); attitude markers (*unfortunately*); and commentary (direct addresses to a reader, such as the example above by Stephen J. Gould) (83–85). As Vande Kopple describes it, metadiscourse helps readers to navigate the text, providing explicit instructions for how to take and what to do with a message.[3]

It is worth pointing out how much written metadiscourse talks about the activities of reading and writing—the interpretive acts that are under way. Consider the following two examples, one that Vande Kopple cites and another from John Deely's *Introducing Semiotic*. I have italicized words and phrases that take their meaning from the acts of reading and writing.

> *In this section two competing hypotheses* about what features are initially missed during the acquisition of spatial adjectives *will be*

reviewed. Following *this review,* the missing-feature theory itself *will be put to a test and will be found* wanting. *In the next section a revision* of the missing-feature theory *will be developed.* (Carey 275)

In order to advance our investigation, we have to *take leave at this point* of the influence of Boethius on the Latin ages *in order to see them also in the light of* developments novel or indigenous to that post-classical period of, as it were, homogeneously Latin philosophizing. *Let us begin with a division* of the objects of knowledge that is both characteristic of and more indigenous to the middle ages, *and highly instructive for our purposes.* . . . (Deely 23)

This language is not, strictly speaking, about the text. It is about "what is going on here," the intellectual enterprises that writer (and any comprehending reader) are up to: sectioning, reviewing, testing, finding, revising, developing, investigating, taking leave, seeing, dividing, instructing—that is, the business of writing and reading. This sort of language is an explicit reminder of the active, constructive cognitive acts that infuse and bring sense to written discourse and of the writer's awareness that a reader is doing things at the other end. While there is illocutionary force in such declarations as "[I am] reviewing" or "[I am] advancing the investigation," we might call these speech acts "literacy acts" as well, as they refer to enterprises that people especially use writing and reading to carry out and that make up the intersubjective accomplishments of writing and reading. In addition, the writer is not the sole proprietor of these illocutionary declarations; in declaring them, a writer makes them part of the joint endeavor. And, more often than not, these declarations acknowledge retroactively a joint endeavor that already is going on: they serve primarily to confirm the status of current understanding.

Metadiscourse, as I mentioned earlier, is perhaps the greatest eruption of involvement-focus in texts, but many other aspects work quietly to maintain the grounds of the we. Communicative dynamism (how "the news" of a text is managed and moved) is especially pertinent here. Research on given-new and theme-rheme chaining shows that the structural nature of written texts manifests not only grammatical order but social sensitivity. How a writer chooses to distribute information across a discourse is an index to the writer's assessment of what is and can be shared at the moment. The general principle of communicative dynamism is a reminder that even the most literal seeming message, the sheerest propositional statement that is the hallmark of exposition, will always be about more than it is ostensibly about. It will always carry a message of involvement along with its propositional message, a message about the state of the we.

For instance, writers select and order given and new information on the basis of the knowledge they can assume to be sharing here-and-now with a reader and what they want to designate as "news" for a reader. The origin of given information can come from various regions of a writer-reader relationship. It may arise from the grounds that writer and reader share by virtue of common membership in a society. Consider, for instance, the following opening sentences from news stories in the *New York Times:*

> Secretary of State George P. Shultz is taking his medium-range arms experts to Geneva for an intense effort to resolve verification issues blocking approval of the new arms accord, Administration officials said today. (Gordon)

> One of the most prominent Soviet cultural figures forced into exile for challenging artistic orthodoxy has returned to Moscow this week to help stage a play at a theater he founded. (Fein)

The grounds that allow the first report to designate Secretary of State George P. Shultz as given information are the same ones that make it inappropriate to start off the second report directly with the name of Yuri Lyubimov, who is the banished Soviet artist that the story refers to. People who know without being told that Shultz is Secretary of State for the United States also are assumed to know which arms accord is "the new" one, to know that the paragraph refers to nuclear weapons agreements (and not a controversy about the appropriate lengths of certain limbs) and to know what is meant by Administration officials and why they are appropriate spokespeople for the activity of George P. Shultz. The whole paragraph speaks of a reader who already has a good idea of what is going on here by virtue of civic experience and knowledge of prior political events.

More commonly, of course, a writer's choice of given information comes from more intimate grounds: those established through the history of the specific text-in-progress. This accounts for the common pattern of new information becoming given information. In the following passage "nature" undergoes such a transformation: "Among the conventions of the more traditional verse in England and the United States throughout the nineteenth century was, obviously, the use of **nature** or landscape as subject matter, setting, symbol, or metaphor. **Nature** is almost omnipresent in this poetry. . . ." (Perkins 4).

Patterns of given and new are not limited to strict repetition of lexical tokens. Frequently "given" designations summarize whole passages. Consider the following passage from George Steiner's essay on Sylvia Plath:

> It is fair to say that no group of poems since Dylan Thomas' *Deaths and Entrances* has had as vivid and disturbing an impact on English critics and readers as has *Ariel.* Sylvia Plath's last poems have already passed into legend as both representative of our present tone of emotional life and unique in their implacable, harsh brilliance. Those among the young who read new poetry will know "Daddy," "Lady Lazarus," and "Death & Co." almost by heart, and reference to Sylvia Plath is constant where poetry and the conditions of its present existence are discussed.
>
> **The spell** does not lie wholly in the poems themselves. (295)

"The spell" appears as given information, even though technically "spell" has not appeared as a previous lexical token. Though only an implied given, it is made strong by the definitive article "the," which says there is no question about which spell is referred to. "The spell" can appear as given because it is, in fact, the tacit discourse topic of the moment. It says that what this passage has been (implicitly) about is "the spell" of Plath's poetry—what all those earlier local sentences add up to is a demonstration of "the spell." "The spell" also is, cohesively speaking, an instance of endophoric reference, directing readers back, Halliday and Hasan would say, to find what "the spell" stands for in some earlier part of the text, thereby providing a strong textual tie between parts (33). Halliday and Hasan (284–91) might also point out the collocation of "the spell" with its semantic cousins in the previous paragraph, "legend" as well as "vivid" and "disturbing," which, in retrospect, take on the semantic tinge of entrancement. Finally, we could say that "the spell" does not merely—and not mainly—function to point backward at an established discourse topic but serves as a pivot into a new topic. Steiner's essay goes on to discuss Plath's life and death. So, while "the spell" provides low communicative dynamism in terms of where the discourse has been, it has some oomph in terms of where the discourse is going. It provides that necessary running start by which Steiner can change the subject.

Structurally speaking, then, "the spell" is a busy little phrase, and in the conventional view, it is busy performing the very functions that realize textual autonomy and self-reference. The phrase ties the text up and to itself. But the very multiplicity of its roles invites a reappraisal, one that I hope will show the deep involvement-focus of this ordinary textual tie, and its actual reference out—to the acts of writing and reading.

The reappraisal begins with a shift in perspective, from treating a text as a static, structural artifact to considering how a text functions for writer at the point of composing and reader at the point of reading. How, the question becomes, can a text be described from an "on-line" perspective, as it is coming over the horizon for writer and reader? And what is the significance of "the spell" from such a perspective?

For one thing "the spell" indicates that writer and reader have just accomplished a generalization. The whole previous paragraph has now been publicly gisted into the label "the spell." Thus the phrase does not merely refer to the sentences in the previous paragraph; it refers to the cognitive acts that writer and reader have just performed. It says "we are now representing all of that as 'the spell.' "

Reading research describes the processes by which readers form and revise the upshot of a text by deleting or combining lower-level bits. Van Dijk and Kintsch, among others, have offered an inventory of these various cognitive moves, suggesting their applicability to both composing and construing texts. Here we can see how a generalizing move is signaled between writer and reader, saying, in effect, "mission accomplished." In this way texts are always talking about the publicly accomplished cognitive acts that are informing them.

Considering how aspects of text function for writers and readers-in-the-act complicates standard divisions between message-focus and involvement-focus in written discourse. More generally, it questions the prevailing view that literate language is detached from pragmatic moorings, divorced from a connection to here-and-now participants. "The spell" would not technically qualify as metadiscourse or as involvement-focused. It is knitted seamlessly into the propositional material of the text and does, among other things, carry a message about the state of affairs in the world. But its potential and success as message originates in writer-reader involvement. It is meaningful only for those who are here, now with the writer at this point in the text. Its meaning is as situational and ad hoc as any gesture by a speaker.

The involvement-focus of the phrase derives largely from its covert reference to the cognitive processes of reading and writing, the cognitive presence of writer and reader, together. "The spell" designates an act of mind as much as an effect of Plath's poetry. We can appreciate how much the underlying cognitive act ("let us generalize") has to be considered part of the meaning of "the spell" by thinking about poor readers and their problems of comprehension. A struggling reader, bogged down in line-by-line decoding, fails to accomplish the gisting and generalizing of better readers. Comprehension falters in a mass of unordered details. To maintain a sense of Steiner's essay, readers not only have to decode "the spell" but have to understand it as a signal to generalize (or, more accurately, recognize the fait accompli among those who are involved here). "The spell" in this spot carries a meaning that will never be found in a dictionary. Its meaning depends on an understanding, at once more general and more particular, of what is going on here. To be unable to appreciate how a text relates to the people who are writing and reading it is fundamentally to be unable to understand its words.

That is why describing literacy as an ability to separate language from people, to make messages in the absence of involvement, so mischaracterizes literacy and so misdiagnoses literacy failure. As David R. Olson and other strong-text advocates would have it, becoming literate requires unraveling language from human entanglements, being able to lay aside reliance on pragmatic events for meaning, understanding that the words on the page are working irrespective of who you are or who the person is who wrote them. That, Olson says, is the hard realization that literacy requires. But, in fact, the requirement is the very reverse. Learning to read is learning how a text is talking to you about your reading. It is learning that what is appearing in the text has everything to do with you and what you are doing on your end. Rather than learning to disengage from pragmatic events, literacy requires learning how to become purely and attentively entangled.

Writing and involvement. I have been trying to demonstrate how the common features of textuality relate to the cognitive accomplishments of writers and readers in the act. We will look at more of these features below. However, it will be useful at this point to back up a bit and reconsider more generally the nature of involvement as it manifests itself during the processes of writing and reading.

In the legacy of oral-literate contrasts (or contrasts between the oral-like and the literate-like) involvement is always in tension with message. A piece of discourse can concentrate on content (aboutness) or it can zero in on participants and the process of communication. As Deborah Tannen has described it, involvement and message work like a seesaw in all discourse. When involvement-focus rises, message-focus necessarily recedes.

But as the example above was meant to suggest, message originates in involvement. In any truly functional piece of discourse, message is, inescapably, an embodiment of involvement. A text feature can and usually does talk about the world and about "what we are up to" at the same time. Thus, the dichotomy of involvement and message does not hold up from a functional, on-line perspective.

In fact, the other partner on the seesaw with involvement is not message but silence or inaction. To speak, to listen, to read, to write is overarchingly to attend, to be involved. To undertake writing at all is to send the involvement seat on the seesaw way up. Writing, from this perspective, is excruciatingly involving because it requires so much of a human being's attention. Part of the normal reluctance to write is that reluctance to get so involved.

There is also something about writing that is extremely intimate. The permanence of writing gives it a high degree of particularity and uniqueness. Each text, even someone's encyclopedia entry, is one of a kind. It would be hard to imagine two writers ever spontaneously composing identical texts, even mundane ones. In conversation, on the other hand, we all recycle familiar topics and anonymous cliches, repeating the same familiar morning greetings, for instance, as we move from street to elevator to hallway. Now, some would say this is evidence of social solidarity and commonality, the very soul of the involvement of which many oral-literate frameworks speak. But there is another kind of involvement, the kind bred of keen, concentrated, and ongoing commitment to a channel of exchange. That is the kind of involvement that writing and reading typically require. And this breeds a special writer-reader solidarity that is maintained over much wider swatches of discourse than is typical of conversation. You cannot just change the subject or casually saunter off for new conversational partners when you are writing. You are in it with your reader for the duration. This involvement becomes an overriding influence, causing a lot of what is hard about composing and creating much of what we recognize as textualness.

Written discourse feeds on a developing writer-reader history. Meaning for both writer and reader emerges—and can only emerge—from a shared and increasingly intimate ground that both can lay claim to. It is a ground comprised of what we (writer and reader) both know is the case right now: that which constitutes our joint awareness, as made possible through the joint experience of the developing text.

A Note on "Audience," "Persona," and "Implied Reader"

So far in this discussion I have been deliberately trying to differentiate *the reader* from *the audience* and *the writer* from *persona*—a distinction that is admittedly hard to pinpoint, especially as all of these "presences" enter into actual acts of writing and reading. The things that writer and reader do to maintain an exchange cannot easily be divorced from the rhetoric of the scene (as the passage from Gould demonstrated). This issue is further complicated by disagreements about concepts like "audience." A major question for theorists and researchers in composition is exactly what constitutes audience awareness and to what extent writers invent audiences out of their knowledge of abstract textual conventions. This contemporary debate reaches at least as far back as Ong's "The Writer's Audience Is Always a Fiction," which argues for the abstraction of the construct and comes closest to what literary theorists have called the "implied" or "model" reader. The "implied" reader is usually identified with textual conventions that embody a role for the reader to play, in other words, "the reader in the text," while Eco has described the "model" reader as the construct a writer uses to generate a text.[4] These sorts of constructs are often enabled by larger cultural contexts that a writer can assume to share with a contemporary audience.

Because literary studies have not really been concerned theoretically or empirically with writing and authorship, it is somewhat difficult to translate these discussions into the composition debate. Rhetoric and composition treat audience more directly from a writer's viewpoint but, even so, from a wide range of perspectives: from literal views of a preexisting, demographic audience (say, the school principal or readers of a certain age, income, educational level, knowledge base, and so on) to more sophisticated versions, such as Douglas Park's, which present audience as a set of interests that can be aroused by the moves that a text makes. Other theorists (like Augustine and Winterowd; and Nystrand) describe the author-audience relationship in terms of pragmatic contracts, megarules for procedures that are meant to balance conflicting interests or states of knowledge. Empirical descriptions of the generative role of audience have been supplied by Flower and Hayes ("Cognition of Discovery") and Berkenkotter, among others. Ede and Lunsford have complicated the picture by suggesting that a writer's sense of audience shifts throughout composing and that writers address many simultaneous audiences who surge into consideration at different points in the process (also see Roth). In most cases, though, a writer's audience is construed as an abstraction, a hypothetic construct, a creation either of authors or texts or, as some reader-response scholars might say, a construction of readers themselves.[5]

The same sorts of complications turn up in discussions of persona. Walker Gibson, drawing on commentary by Ong and Susan Sontag, explores how the word "persona" captures both the artifice and detachment of the mask and the directness and presence of the voice (76–85). As with audience, the question is how much "persona" is an abstraction and hypothetical construction—an implication of text that becomes more than or other than what the writer intends. When Gibson writes that "To catch the particular accent of the speaking voice in a piece of writing is . . . one of our primary obligations as readers" (31), he seems to describe a direct intersubjective awareness unaltered by the move from an oral to written medium. Yet clearly persona is a rhetorical artifice, a creation of words, and Gibson stresses the role-playing quality of persona in which, quoting Sontag, "The mask is the face" (84). (Also see Roger Cherry's useful essay on ethos and persona.)

Treatments of audience and persona are valuable for emphasizing human *relationship* and its role in producing and understanding language. To adopt a persona, as Gibson shows, is to implicate the other; to address an audience is to implicate a self. That is why, despite Ricoeur's assertion mentioned earlier, written language can never escape the "dialogical situation."

However, while the notions of audience and persona make an important contribution to an understanding of involvement and discourse, they nevertheless entail an abstraction. They are a step removed from the actual writer and reader. Although originating in oral rhetoric, persona and audience, in their abstraction, support the view of literate experience as detached and impersonal. Participants in literate exchange are seen, in a sense, as retroactive projections of texts. Writer and reader must contemplate each other into existence within the confines of a text world.

What I am trying to convey with an emphasis on "the wè," however, might best be thought of as aspects of discourse that belong neither to audience nor persona but to *both* the writer and the reader as actual presences at the scene of language. "Weness" arises from the mutual recognition that someone is working to write a text and to read a text. Those enterprises are enabled by a developing history of involvement that is a sign not of the other but of the both, and it is this unfolding history that *enables* the constructions of audience and persona to proceed. The emergent ground of the we is a reminder that the writer-reader relationship is not merely one of antagonism or mismatch or role-playing but one of common orientation to reality.

"Audience awareness" as it is usually invoked, pertains to the rhetorical struggles of writing, the need to balance usually conflicting interests or knowledge states of writer and reader. It accounts for how a writer may proceed in an argument or an explanation, considering or accommodating the perspectives and states of knowledge of others in the world, making textual decisions accordingly. Awareness of the we is a more specific orientation. It accounts for the basis by which argument or explanation can be carried out in the first place. It is a more fundamental, enabling awareness of a particular here-and-now shared state of affairs. Thus, it is far more concrete than audience. Writers have a good idea about how their readers have been spending their time since taking up the text. They have been traveling the same public territory as the writer. The reader is a specific and unique presence. It is the reader of *this* text and the reader at *this* moment in the text. Awareness of the we develops less from schematic discourse rules or genre conventions than from the felt cognitive presence of the both, right here, right now, so far, in this spot. The "striking individual variation" that Linda Flower has observed in the unfolding acts of writing, descriptions of the "local event" and the "current meaning" that writers attend to, the obviously idiosyncratic methods of readers as reported in reader-response studies, all testify to the influence of the particular, dynamic grounds of the we in shaping literate cognition.[6]

I am also suggesting that the presence of writer at work and reader at work permeates written language to a degree that may be underestimated. Sometimes the presence of "the one who is writing" and "the one who is reading" erupts in direct ways, as in the passage by Gould cited earlier or in this odd little passage from a short story, "It" by Theodore Sturgeon: "Cory glanced at the corner behind the wood box where Alton's rifle usually stood, then made an *unspellable,* disgusted sound and sat down to take off his heavy muddy boots" (104, italics mine).

The use of the word "unspellable" reinforces the fictional role of the narrator as a faithful witness reporting on a scene as best he can, so in that sense one can say it contributes to persona. But "unspellable" also refers to the unique acts of writing and reading; it is a reminder that somebody is writing that sentence and somebody is reading it. Use of that word is made possible only through the direct and uniquely literate relationship of the writer and the reader and an awareness of what they are doing here.

Discussions of audience or implied reader frequently emphasize the power of text to create illusions of relationships. For instance, definitive uses of "the" as in "the corner behind the wood box" make the reader an intimate presence in the fictional scene, someone inside "the" room where this action is taking place and familiar with "the wood box." According to Ong and others, these sorts of textual tricks, whether in fiction or nonfictional writing, are what make the role of the reader so contrived—even coerced. The role of the reader is fashioned out of the gap between the circumstances of the "real" reader who is, of course, not there and his or her willingness to participate in the coercion—to perform the intersubjective inferences that are presumed in such textual constructions. These contrivances or coercions are at the heart of the "as ifness" that permeates fictional writing and figure quite centrally in the "alternative" or "possible" worlds of expository writing as well.[7]

However, I want to argue for a different interpretation of these aspects of text, not as carved-out features of a relationship that an eventual reader is expected to "play" into—a "slot" in the text—but rather as liberties sanctioned by a relationship already accomplished (and still developing). These liberties are sanctioned by what writers know about how the joint enterprises of writing and reading work and their sense of a developing shared history, a joint writer-reader presence at the scene of the text itself. Two important shifts in perspective lie behind this argument. First, it requires abandoning a "strong" view of a text as a kind of set of instructions or "score," as in musical score, that a writer fashions and a reader activates. Text features such as the definite articles cited above—and others to be considered in more depth shortly— do not so much *precipitate* involvement as they *register* or index an involvement already accomplished or assumed to be in place by a writer *who needs that involvement in place in order to keep composing.* This becomes clear when we adopt the second shift in perspective: the text is not merely a product of writing but the dynamic, public grounds upon which the work of writing (and reading) take place. The emerging text is the means by which a writer or reader maintains a grip on reality. We need to see better how text features relate to that tenuous intersubjective undertaking—how they are outcomes of underlying attachment in literate experience. This attachment at one level is an allegiance to and recognition of the ongoing reader-writer history, that which we together have established so far. At another it is an attachment at the level of basic orientation. Only by staying attached, only by staying oriented to "what is going on here between us" can a writer or reader proceed in a sensible way.

"What Are We Calling This?"
The Procedure of Labeling

Perhaps the most basic work of writing is deciding what to call things. It is interesting that a chief difference between inner and outer speech is that inner speech frequently has no explicit subject. It is mainly predication.[8] To make a subject is to take that first step into publicness— to initiate the means of sharing. Naming something in writing is to give it over to the grounds of the we. The very designation makes it jointly owned and jointly controlled. In that sense, labeling has an important function in the forward motion of composing. It is not merely the responsibility of a writer preparing proper "reader-based" prose (Flower 1979). It serves as a crucial factor in keeping writing going by pushing open the public horizons from which a writer must work, enabling writing at the same time it constrains it. To give something a name is automatically to take most of the other potential names away. And labeling not only designates an entity but designates the label as well, affiliating the two at least for the duration of a textual exchange.

Labels are indispensable evidence of an evolving writer-reader history, indexes to where the writer and reader have been together. Ethnomethodologists get at the intersubjective significance of this aspect of language with the term "indexical expression" (Bar-Hillel; Garfinkel). An indexical expression is a kind of semantic tip of the iceberg, a phrase behind which lie whole complexes of events and experiences.

"Watergate," "the '60s," and "writing-across-the-curriculum" are common examples. Indexical expressions essentially say "you fill it in." The reference is less to a specific set of events or things than it is to the knowledge that those events or things *are already shared.* Jargon of any sort has this indexical nature, which is why jargon is so frustrating to outsiders. They cannot fill it in. For the same reason, it is often impossible to provide an outsider with a full and adequate explanation of jargon. One has the same problem when a young person asks, "What's Watergate?"

The important fact about indexical expressions is that they point to "us," to a relationship "we" have by virtue of a common experience. Their reference is to an involvement. That is why people are caught up by titles, those labels of labels. Catchy titles draw us in to the extent to which we can imagine the axis of involvement that they promise. A title, in more ways than one, is a preview of a coming attraction.

Written texts are rife with indexical expressions, which carry the metacommunicative message "you fill it in." Indexical expressions are liberties that writers take by virtue of an intimate relationship with their readers.

Consider the following, quite typical explanatory passage from an article about a method of training writing teachers that concentrates on their own development as writers. I will need to quote at length to demonstrate the development of its indexicals:[9]

> The National Writing Project derives from the Bay Area Writing Project, which was the first to formalize a teaching and in-service model based on how one learns to write. Commonly called the "Process Model," its premise is that fluency must be fostered first, and control second. As a training model, this means that the process of developing a composition will be emphasized over its product features. Class time will be devoted to such activities as brainstorming, topic generating, categorizing, nonstop writing, and peer group response. Control of the language is learned through individual or group work that attends to revision, mechanical correctness, formal connections among ideas, grammatical effectiveness, vocabulary development, manuscript features, and spelling.
>
> In the NWP in-service model these classroom practices are typically addressed in an intense 3–5-week summer institute in which teachers write and share in editing/response groups, publish their

own writing in class books, create demonstration lessons for their colleagues, read current research and articles in journals, discuss issues and concerns in the teaching of composition, and respond to presentations by project directors and consultants. This institute format was implemented in the school district where this study was conducted.

Virtually every study of teachers who have participated in NWP training indicates that teachers show striking improvement in their attitudes about themselves as writers and as teachers of writing. . . . (Pritchard 52)

This passage begins by bringing into the text some indexical expressions that already operate somewhere else in the real world, namely the "National Writing Project," the "Bay Area Writing Project" and the "Process Model." If anything, this passage aims to fill in an uninformed reader about the activities associated with these labels. But in the process the writer can increasingly exploit the filled-in reader by turning around and saying "now, you fill in." So the text develops its own set of indexical expressions, such as "the NWP in-service model," "these classroom practices," "this institute format," and "NWP training," which are all labels whose meanings are accomplished in the ongoing writer-reader history. They are labels whose meaning comes into being by virtue of writer and reader progress through the unfolding text. They are enabled— from both the writer's perspective in composing and the reader's perspective in comprehending—by a having been there together. It is interesting to note another indexical expression, "this study," which means "the study I am writing about here and you are reading about here." It is a reference to another dimension of the writer-reader relationship, not tied locally to the experience of this passage but to their roles in general as writer of article and reader of article.

In conventional treatments of written discourse, these labels would, of course, be considered aspects of textual explicitness, the full-dress lexicalizations that make texts autonomous. But from a process-centered perspective, phrases like "this institute format" or "NWP training" are extremely implicit gestures. Their meaning is not fixed in the text but is accomplished, particularly and dynamically, out of the grounds of the we-who-are-here-now.

The intersubjective origins of labeling suggest a reinterpretation of some of the research on parent-child book reading. Many researchers have remarked on the ubiquitous "naming" that goes on when parents read storybooks with very young children. Children are prompted to name objects in pictures or to find important labeling words in texts. Some researchers interpret this early emphasis on labeling as a lesson in objectifying and decontextualizing—the first moves in a detached, literate strategy (see Heath and Thomas; also Olson, " 'See! Jumping' "). But we could see it more profitably as an initial lesson in metacommunication—demonstrating to children how to claim the mutual terms by which literate exchanges proceed, a heightening of intersubjective awareness.

In fact, once this crucial change in perspective is allowed, much of the normal apparatus that we associate with stand-alone texts can be appreciated as part of the cognitive accomplishments of writing and reading. To push even further into this functional 'frontier, I want to claim that *all* textual cohesion is about involvement.

Cohesion and the We

Lexical cohesion, including some of the endophoric references we have already examined, is traditionally treated as classic textness. Halliday and Hasan attribute cohesion to what they call the "textual" function, relating neither to ideas nor to participants but to the powers of texts to relate to themselves (26–27). Cohesion allows texts to self-adhere, to help, in the case of written texts, to hold a message together in its travels across time and space. Lexical cohesion stablizes texts and contributes to autonomy by fixing text irrespective of writer or reader. Cohesion exemplifies the capacities of language-on-its-own in its sheerest glory.

But this reputation has been derived primarily from analysis of finished texts, searches for patterns in static artifacts. One can take a pencil and trace lexical reiteration, pronoun reference, and other devices by which texts point back and forth and usually in at themselves. But tracing such structural patterns in language-on-its-own is like coming upon the scene of a party after it is over and everybody has gone home, being left to imagine from the remnants what the party must have been like.

I have been arguing in this chapter for a view of texts that is based on how they are coming over the horizon for writer and reader, a view which provokes these sorts of questions: What allows a writer to repeat a word, to use a pronoun reference or some other form of lexical substitution? What is accomplished when cohesion is invoked? What is the writer "trading on" when cohesion happens?

Cohesion is another aspect of the shared history of writer and reader.

It refers to something that the two already have accomplished jointly by being involved with something together. A cohesive device says "you know what I mean" or better "we know what I mean." Cohesion says "we are in this thing together." It functions as an indexical expression of previous experience, of previously accomplished understanding. It trades necessarily on writer-reader involvement. It is a mark of intimacy, in Deborah Tannen's words, "a metamessage of rapport" ("Relative Focus" 125).

Consider, for example, the following paragraph from "The Process of Individuation" by Jungian psychologist M.-L. von Franz. The example is already violently taken out of its place in the writer-reader history, which has been going on for some sixty-seven pages. Von Franz is discussing the lapis stone as an important symbol of Self. He writes:

> The fact that this highest and most frequent symbol of the Self is an object of inorganic matter points to yet another field of inquiry and speculation: that is, the still unknown relationship between what we call the unconscious psyche and what we call "matter"— a mystery with which psychosomatic medicine endeavors to grapple. In studying this still undefined and unexplained connection (it may prove to be that "psyche" and "matter" are actually the same phenomenon, one observed from "within" and the other from "without"), Dr. Jung put forward a new concept that he called *synchronocity*. This term means "a meaningful coincidence" of outer and inner events that are not themselves casually [*sic*] connected. The emphasis lies on the word "meaningful." (226)

Not untypically, the first lines of the paragraph function to maintain attention to shared matters that the author is announcing are still relevant here: the big one, Self, of course, which is the topic of von Franz's essay; "field[s] of inquiry and speculation," which have been of some current local interest; and "this highest and most frequent symbol," the lapis, which was introduced in the immediately previous paragraph. These items are "in mind" for writer and reader and von Franz is confirming that they should be kept in mind. Among cohesive devices, according to Halliday and Hasan's inventory, this passage uses lexical reiteration (*matter, psyche, meaningful*); a good deal of substitution (*this . . . symbol, this . . . connection, [t]his term*); and ellipsis (*one . . . and the other*). Collocation, the clustering of semantic relatives, rounds out the main cohesive moves (the pattern of *speculation, unknown, mystery, undefined, unexplained*; and *from 'within'* and *from 'without'* with *synchronocity*).

This passage could serve as a fine example of how texts achieve autonomy, as each sentence seems to nest onto the previous one, moving the message inexorably along by the use of exacting lexical ties. Message-meaning appears to be transacted along the surface of the language. More socially sensitive analyses may note a high degree of glossing (various forms of "in other words" or "that is to say," which amplify rather than add to content and thereby qualify, in Vande Kopple's terms, as metadiscourse). The passage also could be scrutinized for the writer's inferences about readers' prior world knowledge. The first sentence, for example, by embedding as old information "the fact that" lapis is inorganic, assumes a reader already might be mulling that fact and its paradoxical implications for symbolizing human essence. (Von Franz has not raised the inorganic issue previously; it is not part of the "textual context" at this point.) This sentence anticipates a response based on a reader's prior world knowledge that stones are cold and inert. And in fact the rest of the paragraph addresses that response. This is a nice example of how sensitivity to the way public language arouses more than we might want it to (the idea of "lapis") can become a means for a writer to keep up the forward momentum of composing.

Despite all the evidence of involvement that can be dug out of the passage, cohesive ties might continue to dodge serious scrutiny. Cohesion seems so materially part of the text-making function, so tied to the literal text. But as I suggested earlier a repeated phrase or synonym refers not to some retrievable material inscription but to an accomplished experience that is now accessible for social exploitation. Cohesive devices are said to make textual ties but actually they are a *result* of human ties already made between writer and reader.

Returning to the sample passage we can see its fundamentally meta-communicative nature. We can see how much it is really about the act of reading it. What is being made explicit is not a message but the accomplishment of understanding. Collocation and substitution are especially important in this regard in that they indicate a writer's sense of how he or she has just been read, a sense of "O.K., now, how are we going to continue to carry along what I have just said? How shall it be labeled for the purposes of our experience here?" These sorts of cohesive devices especially function to maintain a concurrence about what is going on. In von Franz's case, he writes of a "still unknown relationship," which soon after becomes "a mystery." *Mystery* serves as an ad hoc label. It is a reference to an already accomplished agreement about meaning. Shortly after, "mystery" gives way to "this still undefined and unexplained connection," which describes the manner of mystery that is developing: the kind faced in science, which needs definition and explanation (rather than faith, say) to overcome. This reference says "we are reading *mystery* in this rather secular way." It is not so much a reference to the text as it is a gloss on the reading of it, not unlike what happens in the last sentence of the passage, where, in the quasi-imperative, the author says overtly "read *meaningful coincidence* with the accent on *meaningful*."

When cohesion is taken not as instances of textual self-reference but as indexes to an unfolding writer-reader history, written discourse appears consumed in involvement. In writing, message and metamessage ("what I am saying and what we are doing as a result of it") are often fused within the same lexical items. This merging reflects the fact that writing is more efficient than spontaneous speech because it can be planned and revised. It also reflects the precariousness of the writer-reader channel—the need, through words, to stay in touch at all times about what is going on here.

Involvement and Lexical Precision

Involvement also contributes to the lexical precision and variety that mark formal written texts. An example from our history, yours and mine, will make my point. The term *involvement* has special status in this discourse to refer to intersubjective elements in writing, reading, and texts and their relevance for thinking about literacy. As a result I have consciously avoided or revised out of this text any nonspecialized, incidental use of the term (as in "involving such and such") as potentially distracting, given the state of our relationship. Such a constriction pertains only for the duration of this discourse; it is a repercussion of having gotten involved in this way. Diversity and specificity in writing frequently arise from such constraints, from a writer's sense that certain phrases become designated, used up, off limits because of what already has transpired. The fixity of the text rather than fixing out the relationships of participants actually raises awareness of that developing involvement. That awareness influences the possibilities writers have for proceeding.

Conclusion

In *Text and Context,* Teun Van Dijk makes a small but profound observation that holds the key to the argument of this chapter. He discusses the various ways that discourse topics are introduced into texts (usually through a pattern of topic and comment) and then notes that references to discourse participants do not need to be explicitly introduced in order to take over as a topic. Reader and writer and arguments about them *always* have topic-function privileges. To me this fact of discourse epitomizes the whole social foundation of writing and reading, revealing the text-artifact as but a thin membrane in these most intersubjective of human projects. A writer can call out to reader at any point and not jeopardize coherence. This says, in effect, that "the we" are always in the foreground of consciousness, providing the basis for all other sense, and that bound up in even the most literal of lexical references is the "undertalk" of those who are present at the scene.

The next chapter will examine some of the rhetorical dimensions of this undertalk, continuing as it does to cast a radically social light on standard textual equipment.

Chapter Four

Rhetorics of Involvement

On the night of October 22, 1986, the New York Mets beat the Boston Red Sox in the fourth game of the World Series to tie the series at two games each. The next day the *New York Times* published a feature story, "There's No Stopping Carter," by sports writer Ira Berkow, the first eight paragraphs of which appear below:

Boston, Oct. 22—After waiting 12 years to get into a World Series, Gary Carter is not about to allow a couple of sore knees, a single sore thumb, a "beat-up" left palm, a dollop of frustration, a soupçon of fatigue and assorted other maladies and inconveniences—like the Boston Red Sox—to interfere with his good time. (1)

This is Gary Carter's 12th full season in the big leagues, and only once, in 1981, had he ever before been in a championship series. He was catching for Montreal, which lost in the playoffs to the Dodgers. (2)

After the Mets lost the first two games of the World Series to the Red Sox, they came back to win Game 3 Tuesday night, 7–1, on the strength of, among other things, two clutch hits by Carter—a double and a single, driving in three runs. (3)

Now, as the Mets went into Game 4, down 2 games to 1, he felt the team's chance against Al Nipper, the Red Sox starter, was strong. (4)

"Nipper hadn't pitched in any of the playoff games against California," said Carter, "and he had a high e.r.a. this season." Nipper's earned run average was 5.38 to go along with his 10–12 record. He said the Mets weren't "taking Nipper lightly, but the general consensus is that we can beat him." (5)

Carter said that John McNamara, the Red Sox manager, was starting Nipper because he didn't want to overwork his aces, Roger Clemens and Bruce Hurst. (6)

"If we win," the Mets' catcher said, "then it's 2–2 and anyone's series. Just the way it was for us against Houston." (7)

But the Mets could not have had such an upbeat approach for Game 4 if they had not survived Game 3. (8)

This article was written for readers who are "involved" with baseball generally and with the Mets' fate in the 1986 World Series particularly. Readers of the first paragraph are assumed to know that Gary Carter is the Mets' catcher (and not, say, an accident-prone baseball fan who has finally managed after twelve years to get tickets to the Series). And the entire story presumes an understanding of professional baseball, with its free use, among other things, of baseball lingo and its frequent oblique references to divisional playoffs. The author's patterns of identification also signal an affiliation with New York Mets' fans, as the story assumes great intimacy with Carter and his teammates while Red Sox figures are carefully designated ("the Red Sox starter," "the Red Sox manager").

But actually the article relies less on readers' particular and partisan knowledge of baseball than it does on readers' tacit ability to manage shifting social relationships, including the one between author and reader, author and Carter, Carter and the Mets, Carter and the Red Sox, and reader and the *New York Times*. Making sense of this article depends heartily on keeping track of who is involved with whom, how, and when.

Consider first what happens in the initial paragraph. The general expectation in reading a news account is that it will convey information about some state of affairs or commentary on that state of affairs by relevant people. This convention is the basis of news objectivity and factivity. Reporters tell what happened, presumably in a way that it would have been told by any similarly disinterested witness. With this general expectation framing the reading, one might begin this article assuming it is a report of Carter's attitude toward his injuries—that he had, in essence, told the reporter "I am not going to let my injuries interfere with my good time." But that expectation begins to be upset upon arriving at the phrases, "a dollop of frustration" and "a soupçon of fatigue." First, they are not phrases a baseball player ordinarily uses. And, second, they signal a shift in an otherwise unadorned list of Carter's physical aches to an explicitly intrusive presence: someone else is looking at Carter.[1] We realize, as readers, that we are being invited to contemplate Carter, together with Berkow, as if Berkow were sitting next to us in the grandstands, nudging our elbow and saying, "Hey, how about that guy Carter!" The pertinent perspective is not Carter's but ours, writer and reader, as onlookers.

For the first three paragraphs, then, Carter is the source of interest but not the source of information. That situation changes, however, at the start of the fourth paragraph when the article shifts to an interview with Carter, and the author adopts a more traditional reportorial role as interviewer. This change in perspective is announced only with the temporal shifter "Now" and the appearance soon after of direct quotes. When Berkow writes, "[Carter] felt the team's chance against Al Nipper . . . was strong," we are no longer to imagine, along with Berkow, what Carter feels but rather to take the statement as something straight from the horse's mouth. The reporter-as-informer (who is present in paragraphs 2 and 3) reappears in paragraph 5 in the gloss on Carter's comments about Nipper's high earned run average. Berkow's elaboration says, in effect, "This is what Carter means by a high e.r.a." or "Carter is justified in those comments about Nipper—look at these stats." (That the focus in paragraph 5 is meant to remain on Carter, not Nipper, registers in the resumption of the "He" for Carter in the next sentence.)

Readers must follow the writer's shift in social perspective—from being another fan in the stands in the first paragraph, to interpretive guide, to reporter of privileged information. Readers have to know the range of Berkow's roles to know how to take the words. And, just as we must adjust our stance toward Berkow as the article proceeds, so must we shift our stance toward Carter, changing from distant contemplators of his public behavior on the field to third-party receivers of his views about the progress of the Series.

Other perspectives also need to be tracked and tended. Paragraph six reports that "Carter said that John McNamara, the Red Sox manager, was starting Nipper because he didn't want to overwork his aces, Roger Clemens and Bruce Hurst." The literal sense of this report is that Carter is serving as spokesman for the manager of the opposite team. By knowing this is an inappropriate and unlikely role, we can understand that Carter is not reporting McNamara's perspective but rather the Mets' perspective on McNamara's motives. Carter is acting as spokesman for the Mets, not the Red Sox manager. This perspective then dissolves in paragraph eight as the reporter is back out of the interview and offering another perspective, that of analyst of the Mets' mood as reflected in Carter's report. Here Berkow glosses the upshot that writer and reader together have been garnering from the interview with Carter: the Mets are in an upbeat mood. Paragraph eight, in other words, is a metacommunicative report. It offers a reading of our reading so far.

There are yet more perspectives to consider. Readers of this October

23, 1986, issue of the newspaper can bring their day-after perspective to the article, knowing that the Mets in fact had won the fourth game, a perspective that was available neither to Carter at the time he gave the interview nor to Berkow at the time he filed his story. (Indeed, had the Mets lost, the story in all likelihood would not have been published.) This raises a second aspect of involvement that is crucial to understanding the article: the several dimensions of time that are referred to. There is the general now that represents Carter's twelfth season in the big leagues (that is, the now of the 1986 baseball season and, particularly, the ten-day or so now of the 1986 World Series). There is the immediate past of the first three games of the series, which includes "Tuesday." There is the now of the dateline (Oct. 22), the now in which Carter speaks and Berkow writes. And there is the "real world" now of Thursday, October 23, the day of publication, which is after the Mets have played and won Game 4.

The article depends for its tenses, reference, coherence, and significance largely on the assumption that readers are involved in some real time, some of which they share with Berkow and Carter and some of which they do not. That Berkow writes with this awareness registers in the following oddly tensed phrase: "Now, as the Mets went into Game 4," a fusion of present and past, common in written narratives, which only makes sense in terms of the temporal relationship between writer and reader. To understand that tense you have to understand that you are being written to.

As the article demonstrates, one of the fundamental requirements in all reading is deciding quite literally where an utterance is coming from, what sector of experience it orginates from and/or refers to, and what aspect of the author-reader relationship sanctions such a reference. Only by knowing where a statement is coming from can a reader decide what to do with it. This procedure is most pronounced in Berkow's article because perspectives shift so rapidly and with little explicit announcement save for some standard textual conventions, such as paragraphing (which helps greatly in the management of temporal shifts) and quotation marks. Consider once more paragraph 5, where the literal message is so inextricably bound up with who is talking to whom about whom, and where the real message resides in the metacommunicative layer that is getting accomplished between author and reader.

"Nipper hadn't pitched in any of the playoff games against California," said Carter, "and he had a high e.r.a. this season." Nipper's earned run average was 5.38 to go along with his 10–12 record. He said the Mets weren't "taking Nipper lightly, but the general consensus is that we can beat him."

Just to process this paragraph a reader has to grasp Berkow's metacommunicative message in each sentence: "Carter is talking to me." "I am talking to you." "Carter is talking to me." Otherwise, sentence 2 is particularly puzzling and difficult to place. The presence or absence of quotation marks and attribution are the only signals of the changes in information source. A reader also has to surmise that the paragraph is about something other than it is ostensibly about. Literally we would have to say that the paragraph is about Nipper's pitching, because the paragraph reports the part of the Berkow-Carter interview that dealt with Nipper and because the paragraph carries factual content about Nipper's e.r.a. and his status on the Red Sox pitching roster. But, pragmatically, the paragraph is still about the attitude of the Mets, as conveyed by Carter, going into Game 4. The telltale "He" (for Carter) that starts the last sentence says that, for writer and reader, the real focus is still on the Mets' catcher, not the Red Sox pitcher.

The entire article is circumscribed by a joint writer-reader involvement in tracking the Mets' mental outlook. This involvement originates in the wider, real-world relationship of news organ to sports-page reader, in which the media (standing in for the fan) seeks observations and opinions of team players, managers, owners, and others, which, when reported, become grist for fans' predictions and interpretations of a sports event. But this shared writer-reader enterprise is not merely the external occasion prompting Berkow's feature story. It is the very enterprise that brings meaning to the literal words of the text. What the words say cannot be divorced from who is saying them. And what the words mean cannot be divorced from what the writer and the reader are up to together.

This sports feature, temporal, consumable, narrative entertainment, is not, of course, an example of the formal expository essay that is the prototype for most strong-text explanations of literacy and textuality. But, as later analysis will reveal, the process of interpretation required to read it is quite typical of the involvement focus that must be sustained in reading any sort of text. And the centrality of social involvement in literate cognition raises serious challenges to prevailing accounts of both literacy and textuality.

Recall that in strong-text formulations, the transition from the oral to the literate is a transition from meaning based on social relationships to meaning based on semantic relationships. Not merely does the "the what" take precedence over "the who" but meaning is to be deduced from the logical relationships among internal propositions. The relationship that matters in written discourse is the relationship among ideas, and making textual relationships is what makes things so in the text world.

This formula has been used to explain the "texture" of a text as arising from various superordinate and subordinate relationships among its parts. Paragraphs, for instance, are frequently analyzed in terms of the logical and structural standings of the constituent sentences one to another, making textual texture a mixture of general and specific, assertion and evidence, entailment and consequence, and so on.[2] This formula also figures in explanations of the unique nature of written rhetoric, which, according to Olson and others, operates on principles significantly different from oral rhetoric. Written rhetoric, says Olson, functions largely in an illocutionary vacuumn where language, detached from social relationships, goes it alone. The shift in the site of meaning, from a basis in human contact to the logical and semantic resources of opaque written language, is said to foster a distinctly written rhetoric, which emphasizes evidence, stipulation, logic, and completeness of argument. Literate rhetoric will be "audience aware" in that an effective rhetor anticipates beliefs, knowledge, and needs of an intended audience in crafting a text. But the aim, in this view, is to deliver up a finished artifact in which the persuasive power arises from the clarity and logic of the argument and the aptness, reasonableness, and completeness of evidence, all arranged within the well-formed borders of the text. The objectivity that is so valued in this kind of rhetoric is really inseparable from the physically objective text, the "it" that is the focus of a reader's private, silent contemplation and judgment. To derive the meaning of a passage one must recognize these patterns of internally stipulated relationships.

It is for these reasons that logical, categorical thinking is conventionally associated with literacy and why literacy failures are frequently ascribed to failures in logical, abstract thinking. Frank D'Angelo, for example, holds this view. He writes, beginning with an argument familiar from oral-literate contrasts:

> The thinking of preliterate and nonliterate people is concrete, syncretic, diffuse, perceptual, affective, situation-bound, additive,

and digressive, concerned with everyday events, actions, and happenings rather than with abstract ideas. The thinking of literate people tends to be more abstract, discrete, definite, and articulated, consisting of generalizations, deductions, and inferences. . . . What I am suggesting is that one possible reason for the decline in literacy might be related to the incipient or undeveloped forms of literate thinking in some of our students. ("Literacy and Cognition" 104)

Whatever social considerations may go into the making of literate rhetoric, they are pretty much erased from explicit reference, for they are irrelevant to the purposes of public exchange. Literate rhetoric, as so described, is a rhetoric of physical, social, and cognitive detachment, a rhetoric of noninvolvement.

The previous chapter began to develop an alternative explanation of literate orientation as requiring a heightened sense of intersubjective involvement. Readers must be able to see illocutionary presence despite corporeal absence and to see how a text relates to their own presence on the scene, to what they, as readers, are doing moment to moment. Only by maintaining this intimate awareness can readers carry out the work of reading. Authors also trade on this awareness with frequent references, both direct and oblique, to the acts of writing and reading in progress, and with language that indexes the developing history of joint writer-reader accomplishments. This history of public accomplishments becomes an increasingly important grounds of meaning for both participants. Authors, through their texts, also assume intersubjective awareness is in place because often the literal words of a text only make sense in terms of it. The dense appearance of and dependence upon intersubjective involvement in written texts suggests some needed adjustments in prevailing descriptions of literate discourse and what it demands of readers.

My aim in this chapter is to continue to offer an account of textual language and its demands that challenges some of the key provisions in strong-text theories. We will look at the texture of some formal expository discourse to show how it arises not from a set of formal, logical, text-based relationships but from various axes of experience that readers, by virtue of their evolving relationship with the author, are able to draw upon. Formal expository texts move not so much up and down the scale of general to specific but in and out of various perspectives and reference points that readers are expected to monitor and invoke. We also will reconsider what is actually being made explicit in so-called explicit, decontextualized discourse. In strong-text formulas, the movement from utterance to text is a movement away from meaning based in practical action and intersubjective appeal toward meaning fixed by message-dense propositions that together constitute an objective and detached text world. On closer inspection, however, the seemingly stipulative and explicit language associated with formal exposition turns out to refer not to a detached text world but to the here-and-now acts of writing and reading that are under way. Thus, formal exposition appears not as a discourse that obliterates pragmatic meaning but as a discourse that makes pragmatic meaning and the means of its accomplishment *the* conscious concern of both writer and reader. As we will see shortly, the essentially metacommunicative nature of written discourse is especially important in explaining how written rhetoric works.

Literacy and Rhetoric

Consider this opening paragraph from an essay by Loren Eiseley called "Man in the Autumn Light."

The French dramatist Jean Cocteau has argued persuasively about the magic light of the theatre. People must remember, he contended, that "the theatre is a trick factory where the truth has no currency, where anything natural has no value, where the only things that convince us are card tricks and sleights of hand of a difficulty unsuspected by the audience." (*Invisible Pyramid* 119)

How is that first sentence to be read? Literally it declares something about Jean Cocteau, of course. But how do we know that, in this context, the sentence is not really about him? How do we know that although Eiseley chooses to tell us (or remind us of) something about Cocteau that there is more to it than that? Is the sentence, instead, about the "magic light of the theatre"? Certainly the given-new pattern makes that phrase the news of the sentence. Our attention is pointed in that direction. But how do we know that the sentence is not really—or at least not solely—about the magic light of the theatre either? What readers do notice is that the "theatre light" of the opening sentence is related to the "autumn light" of the essay title, an association that begins to accumulate the weight of a possible global theme or topic. Here is a clue to about-ness. But what is the result of that basic act of perception? In making the thematic connection between autumn light and theatre light we must collapse the distinction between the natural and the artificial. As any reader of the full essay will discover, this is a main ingredient in Eiseley's argument. He goes on to assert that what we typically regard as nature is no less contrived and unnatural as the "trick factory" of the theatre. By making a basic decision about how to take the first sentence, readers are "tricked" prematurely into performing the very association that the author, in the next paragraph, will ask us to accept.

If the basic work of reading Eiseley's opening paragraph involves us in accomplishing the rhetorical point, it also involves us in accomplishing rhetorical stance. For if we ask what this whole paragraph really refers to, we see that it is to how Eiseley wants us to read. Consider first which words in this paragraph Eiseley is most responsible for, which parts are most identified with him and draw attention to him. They are "has argued persuasively" and "People must remember, he contended." Everything else in that paragraph belongs to the world and time of Cocteau, to the factivity of his name, his work, his words. But in these two phrases we are given access to Eiseley and the "presentness" of his interpretation. These phrases tell us something about Eiseley: that he finds Cocteau's argument persuasive.

In fact the whole allusion to Cocteau not only sets up a theme for the essay but also is there to represent the writer-reader relationship that Eiseley wants established for the duration of his essay. Just as Cocteau has argued persuasively about the magic light of the theatre, Eiseley will argue persuasively about the magic light of the cosmos. This introduction announces to readers that they are in the presence of argument and contention, that the contention is over matters of naturalness and contrivance, and that Eiseley views his readers, like Cocteau, as an "unsuspecting audience" who must be reminded of the things his essay will go on to say. All of the words that Eiseley directly authors in the introduction speak of the intersubjective relationship through which this exchange is to be accomplished.

Knowing how to handle that relationship is, in fact, what distinguishes expert readers from so-called novice readers. In an interesting set of studies that have remarkable parallels with process profiles of writers, Vipond and Hunt compared a group of expert readers with more typical, college-aged student readers ("Point Driven"). They found the student readers were content-driven in their approach to texts. The students concentrated on understanding and remembering information in the same literal, propositional form in which a text rendered it. The expert readers, on the other hand, were "point driven." As they read they attempted to determine what an author was trying to do, especially what an author was trying to do to them, and their comprehension of the text was accomplished in these terms. (Haas and Flower, in their profiles of expert readers, call this strategy "rhetorical reading.") Expert readers know how to transform a text into an episode in which they are centrally involved. Like expert writers, they regard literate experience as a complex speech act.

In one sense the differences between the expert and nonexpert (i.e., student) readers in these studies can be explained in cultural terms: the two groups simply perceive the activity of reading differently. Students, used to being examined on the content of assigned texts, understandably will read to preserve content even as they try to master it. How students read reflects the circumstances in which they read. Likewise, the expert readers, who in such studies tend to be scholars, teachers, and writers, usually read to help themselves fulfill these other roles. Reading for them is a transformative activity in practical, real-life terms. So, not surprisingly, the actual cognition of their reading is geared in this way. Point-driven readers understand that they have a place in the progress of a text and that the meaning of a text is fused to their presence on the scene, to what they are doing as well as what the author is doing. This is a realization that is rarely available directly in literal inscription and, unfortunately, rarely encouraged in reading practices in school.

While expert and novice readers differ largely in terms of the expectations and experiences that they bring to reading in the first place, the way they treat a text also needs to be considered. Clearly the two groups "take" the words of the same text differently. Where nonexperts may read a propositional statement, experts read a metamessage from the author, a provocation, a confirmation, an anticipated response, an intimate reference to "what is going on here." Expert readers learn to hear the undertalk that aids them both in comprehending and critically interpreting what they read. Recent reading theory and research have stressed how much readers bring to a text in terms of background knowledge, expectations, inferences, and so on—how much, that is, readers must read into a text in order to make it make sense. But the process could just as well be described in terms of what different readers pick up from a text. The mobilization of appropriate knowledge, inference, and hypotheses that marks the processes of better readers begins with how they take the words before them. Good readers accomplish the work of reading more fluently because they perceive that they are being talked to about that work, and they discern the relationship between metacommunicative references and the "the point" of a text. That is why to understand how a text works, one has to understand how reading (and readers) work.

Textual Hierarchy and Orders of Involvement

Conceiving of textuality in terms of logical and semantic relationships among parts is a cornerstone of prevailing descriptions of literate discourse. And it is crucial to the equation of literacy with antisocial orientation. As Chapter One explained, written discourse is seen to have gathered to itself powers of semiotic autonomy by developing fixed and impersonal conventions of genre, grammar, and syntax. With these resources, textual language could become an independent operator, irrespective of particular contexts of time, place, and social relationships. For text users, according to this view, the new semiotic possibilities of written language require changes in interpretive procedure. Readers must be able to recognize the conventions of genre as a formal, abstract replacement for setting and be willing and able to capitulate to the stipulations of the very words of the text. They must accept reference as largely endophoric and the pertinent context as semantic, since written words, in this view, take their meaning from syntactic and semantic relationships to other words around them. Readers must be able and willing to rely on abstract, deductive reasoning as an avenue for resolving problems of meaning.

As with other aspects of strong-text characterizations, however, this description does not accurately account for the processes of interpretation that most texts, including (and maybe especially) formal expository ones, demand. The problem for readers is not usually puzzling out the formal relationships among adjacent parts but keeping track of the complicated perspectives that are often laid side by side in a text with only the subtlest indications of change. As a text progresses it develops a certain relationship to a topic, may at the same time be reporting the relationships of others to the topic, while simultaneously maintaining the writer-reader relationship through which the entire discussion is being managed. Textual relationships are less logical than they are social: they arise out of recognizing what is mine, yours, ours, his, hers, theirs, its. But especially what is ours—because reference in written discourse is always *in reference to* the participants, writer and reader, and to their joint business at hand.

By way of example, consider the following paragraph from Berger, Berger, and Kellner's *The Homeless Mind,* a passage of typical, abstract, explicit, and rather dense scholarly writing. The book explores the influence of modern economic and social organizations on human cognition and consciousness, and this particular passage deals with the relationship between the individual and modern bureaucracy. It is necessary to quote at length to capture the various vectors of involvement that a reader must track in order to comprehend this passage.

The encounter with bureaucracy takes place in a mode of *explicit abstraction.* In the discussion of technological production, abstraction was seen to be implied but not necessarily available to the consciousness of the individual engaged in such production at any given moment. By contrast, the abstractness of bureaucracy is typically available to the consciousness of its client (and of course to its practitioner). In other words, there is a general knowledge of the abstract modalities of bureaucracy and at least a very common readiness to play the game by the rules of this abstraction. This fact gives rise to a contradiction: The individual expects to be treated "justly." As we have seen, there is considerable moral investment in this expectation. The expected "just" treatment, however, is possible only if the bureaucracy operates abstractly, and that means it will treat the individual "as a number." Thus the very "justice" of this treatment entails a deeper depersonalization of each individual case. At least potentially, this constitutes a threat to the individual's self-esteem and, in the extreme case, to his subjective identity. The degree to which this threat is actually felt will depend on extrinsic factors, such as the influence of culture critics who decry the "alienating" effect of bureaucratic organization. One may safely generalize here that the threat will be felt in direct proportion to the development of individualistic and personalistic values in the consciousness of the individual. Where such values are highly developed, it is likely that the intrinsic abstraction of bureaucracy will be felt as an acute irritation at best or an intolerable oppression at worst. In such cases, the "duties" of the bureaucrat collide directly with the "rights" of the client— *not,* of course, those "rights" that are bureaucratically defined and find their correlate in the "duties" of the bureaucrat but rather those "rights" that derive from extrabureaucratic values of personal autonomy, dignity, and worth. The individual whose allegiance is given to such values is almost certainly going to resent being treated "as a number." Conversely, groups in which these values have been less firmly established are likely to be less troublesome-clients for bureaucracy. As we shall see later, this potential conflict between bureaucratic consciousness and the value of individual autonomy has far-reaching sociological consequences. (55–56)

The main interpretive issue for readers of this passage is keeping track of whose words are whose. This is necessary both for understanding quite basically what the authors are talking about and for understanding the authors' point that conflict between individuals and bureaucracies arises from what various interested parties call the same experience. Readers not only have to keep track of what the authors say is going on between members of various social groups and the bureaucracy but they also have to keep track of what is going on between the authors and themselves, as these different orders of activities often blend seamlessly and implicitly together in the texture of this text.

The first appeal to these multilines of reference occurs in the very first sentence, where readers have to understand that the italicized words *explicit abstraction* are words that belong to the authors and the reader: the phrase announces what authors and reader together shall be calling what is in the process of being described. Thus, though this first sentence denotes an encounter by some persons with some bureaucracy in some world, what the statement is really about is naming what it is about. And the naming is in relation to the writers and their readers. Readers have to understand that the next sentence too arises from the writer-reader domain, that it refers to their jointly accomplished past, now available as a grounds for mutual interpretation. And they have to realize that while "the discussion of technological production" is syntactically similar to "the encounter with bureaucracy," the meanings of the two phrases arise from distinctively different spheres. The latter is sanctioned by the authors' privilege to refer to events in some world; the former by privilege of reference to interpersonal involvement in the here-and-now world brought about through the acts of writing and reading this text.

Determining whose words are whose becomes part of the explicit rhetorical fabric of the passage. The authors put quotation marks around several key words ("justice," "duties," "rights," "as a number," "alienating") as the words become associated with various competing perspectives. Marking off these words underscores the authors' point that conflict arises from different expectations that different constituencies bring to the bureaucracy. The meaning of these words is not important here, the quotation marks say, only that the words represent conflicting values. Marking off these charged words also allows the authors to maintain (for themselves and for their readers) a certain objectivity toward the scenario they describe. The quotation marks preclude taking sides because they hold all the language up as self-interested and suspect. But, the quoted words do relate to the author-reader project as much as to the clients, bureaucrats, and culture critics, and in that regard they must be taken as nonsuspect, as factual description of a factual situation. Those phrases are there to explicate the authors' definition of "explicit abstraction," to make the point that, although different constituencies bring different expectations to bear upon the bureaucracy, they all share an understanding of the fundamental abstraction of their relationships, an abstraction signaled in such abstract words as "justice" or "duties." The authors are using the same words to explain modern bureaucracy as they are to explain themselves to their readers. Everything is going on at the same time in the same place.

I have belabored the multifunctioning of these metacommunicative marks only to make the point that access to the simultaneity of meanings is through the axis of writer-reader involvement and their joint endeavor. The complexity and density that is typically ascribed to formal written discourse arises not from its capacity to explicate and delineate situations fully, deductively, and independently of participants but from the fact that people typically use written discourse to contemplate complex situations together. A good deal of the "texture" of written discourse is due to that growing entanglement in mutual contemplation. To understand any piece of written discourse, readers have to figure out whose words are whose, whose facts are whose, so that when the authors in the passage above, for instance, say "This fact gives rise to a contradiction," readers understand that "this fact" is *their* fact, an accomplishment of the authors and readers. It belongs to their domain and to their joint enterprise to uncover the "far-reaching sociological consequences" of the conflict under discussion.

Tracking pertinent perspectives not only is necessary simply for decoding a text (if decoding can be called simple) but it is crucial for critically apprehending the biases at work in an author's presentation. For instance, while the passage from *The Homeless Mind* adopts an ostensibly objective stance toward the situation it describes, the authors' choices of reference weight the discussion as a struggle between autonomy-loving individualists and a rather oppressive bureaucracy. Notice, for instance, toward the end of the passage, the thematic focus is on clients of the bureaucracy who esteem individualistic and personalistic values. The "threat" that is being described is a threat the bureaucracy poses *to them*. In the second-to-last sentence, the authors shift their focus to other social groups, groups "in which these values [of personal autonomy] have been less firmly established." To continue a parallel perspective, we would expect the authors then to describe how the bureaucracy appears to this second group. But a shift in perspective happens right in the middle of that sentence, so that the description instead is of how this second group appears to the bureaucracy (as "likely to be less troublesome clients"). This shift in perspective has two immediate rhetorical effects. It emphasizes the oppressiveness of the bureacracy by describing the relationship of both groups in terms of threat. (The values of the first group are threatened by the bureaucracy, and the bureaucracy is nonthreatened—or less threatened—by the values of the second group.) But this perspective also reveals the underlying interest of the authors in the plight of the first group, which, in class terms, is the educated middle class. By structuring out the feelings and reactions of the second group (whose members typically include the working class, minorities, and others outside the mainstream middle class), the authors marginalize the second group and depict the main struggle as one between the bureaucracy and the middle class (of which they and presumably most of their readers are members). The ideological involvement of writer and reader as members of the same cultural group plays an obvious role in this presentation. The passage is not particularly written for people who identify with the second group.

"Text Worlds" and Metacommunicative Reference

One of the chief rationales for a strong-text account of literate discourse is that it explains the method by which written language is used to explore "possible" or "alternative" worlds. Where reference in speech remains physically tied to a speaker and the commonsense world that it indexes, writing is said to achieve genuine autonomous representation outside the confines of normal social bonds and normal social reality. Texts appear from this view as sets of instructions for building and contemplating resistant worlds, organized in accordance with semantic stipulations and achieved by willful detachment from what one usually shares with others. Reference is uniquely decontextualized in this view, for textual words point only in and around the textual world of their own fabrication. If references to the real world do enter, they are susceptible to transformation, bracketed treatment, critical reorganization. This is what makes texts strong and what makes literacy, in prevailing descriptions, a solitary and alienated experience—for the text world is independent, uninhabited, a detached creation of language on its own. It would be difficult to deny the central function of written discourse in contemplating fictional, alternative, and theoretical realities. The power of literate language to transform ordinary vision is a chief reason people turn to it, as writers and readers, in its many genres (and a chief reason why literacy has been, throughout history, politically controlled). The question, though, is by what interpretive avenues the so-called text world is realized. This chapter has examined and found unsatisfactory some prevailing explanations of that process, namely, a reliance on literal inscription and an investment in logical relationships as a way to resolve questions of meaning. Neither can well account for the interpretive procedures that literates (especially skilled ones) invoke during acts of writing and reading. And neither can faithfully account for the dense appearance of metacommunicative language in formal exposition, language that is only comprehensible in terms of its relationship to the people who are writing and reading it. In fact, what is typically described as the most formal, explicit, abstract, logical, and detached expository discourse is actually discourse that refers more and more exclusively to the cognitive activities of writer and reader together. It is discourse that approaches pure involvement focus, as it focuses more and more intimately on the process by which intersubjective understanding is being accomplished.

B. F. Skinner's theoretical essay "What Is Man?" serves as a useful example here because it squarely qualifies as an exploration of alternative possibilities. In it Skinner argues for replacing what he calls the "autonomous agent" theory of human behavior with environmentalism or what he calls a "contingencies of reinforcement" theory. The essay begins by observing why environmentalism has had difficulty taking hold (because of a lack of understanding of the environment itself) and then goes on methodically to translate familiar aspects of the "autonomous agent" theory into environmental explanations. In the conventional view, one might say that Skinner sets out to replace one model world (based on free agency) with another one (based on environmental reinforcement), and that reference is to the elements of that transformation. But to understand the essay, readers have to see that though the discussion is ostensibly about a current situation in human behavior theory, Skinner is really talking about the situation here, now, as it stands between himself and the reader. The descriptions of a model world are also descriptions of the discussion in progress, and the key transformations that Skinner advocates are transformations that must be accomplished by the reading mind.

So, for instance, in the following passage, as Skinner addresses the failures of what he calls "crude environmentalism," he simultaneously describes what he is doing here, in this essay, and what readers must do also. Comprehending the text, preparing for what is to come next, depends on an ability to read in this double way. (I have italicized the pertinent sentences.)

> Both the enthusiasm of the environmentalist and his usually ignominious failure are illustrated by Owen's utopian experiment at New Harmony. A long history of environmental reform—in education, penology, industry, and family life, not to mention government and religion—has shown the same pattern. Environments are constructed on the model of environments in which good behavior has been observed, but the behavior fails to appear. Two hundred years of this kind of environmentalism has very little to show for itself, and for a simple reason. *We must know how the environment works before we change it to change behavior. A mere shift in emphasis from man to environment means very little.*
>
> *Let us consider some examples in which the environment takes over the function and role of autonomous man.* (*Beyond Freedom and Dignity* 185)

The same words that render a verdict on Owen's social experiments also render metacommunicative directions, announcing Skinner's here-and-now interest in how the environment works and telling us we must understand his argument as more than a mere shift in emphasis. This is a gloss not only of Owen's failures but of a method for reading the essay.

That readers must accomplish the transformations that Skinner proposes is especially obvious in the last sentence quoted above, which offers even more explicit directions for reading. Skinner is not objectively describing a hypothetical world in which an environment wrests power from autononous man. Rather, he is offering readers means to accomplish cognitively the conditions he envisions. To make that sentence make sense, readers have to understand how it is talking to them about what they are supposed to be doing. Likewise, in subsequent passages when Skinner writes, "The explanation shifts from a trait of character to an environmental history of reinforcement" (186) or "An analysis of the environmental circumstances reverses the relation" (186) or "The inner gatekeeper is replaced by the contingencies to which the organism has been exposed and which selects the stimuli to which it reacts" (187), he writes not of activities that are occurring in a hypothetical text world but of activities that a cooperative reader should be in the process of accomplishing: activities of shifting, analyzing, reversing, and replacing. The real subject of all of those sentences is "what we are doing." These references update things in the real world of writer and reader together.

Toward a Redefinition of Literacy and Literate Discourse

I have been attempting to suggest that the nature of textuality generally and the nature of written rhetoric particularly cannot be explained without broad and deep appeal to the social relationship of writer and reader and to the here-and-now acts of writing and reading. Sometimes, as in the case of the newspaper story about Gary Carter, the social relationship is implicitly preestablished in the stereotypic roles of the participants. As we saw, the article depends for its sense on an understanding of the social function of the sports writer vis-à-vis the sports-page reader. The text "trades" on that relationship without much explicit development of it. It is simply in place, circumscribing the whole textual exchange. In more formal, extended expository essays, in which the writer-reader relationship is more ambiguous or open-ended to begin with, more attention may be given to establishing and evolving the basis of exchange and the grounds of involvement simultaneously with the exchange itself.

What has happened now to the characterization of literacy with which we began? As the first chapter demonstrated, the long-standing association of literacy with decontextualization of language has been shaped around models of texts, rather than people. Literacy as literalism, literacy as the way of the text, is itself a kind of literal translation of the characteristics of the archival text into a model of literacy and literacy learning. The most tangible difference between the oral and the literate is the thingness, the separateness of the text. And because literacy has been construed as the ability to meet the demands of this thing, the text, decontextualization (of language, thought, and ultimately self) has come to be synonymous with literacy, just as an inability to decontextualize has come to be synonymous with literacy failure.

In such strong-text characterizations, the development of literacy is tied to the technological development of textuality. As the evolution of the alphabet and subsequently print has been toward stronger powers of preservation, ever finer capacities for exact and autonomous representation, so the human acts of writing and reading have come to be seen primarily as efforts at preserving text. In this formula, writers fortify fixed texts and readers capitulate to that fixity. The nature of texts bequeaths meaning to the acts of writing and reading—not only in the sense of providing the means to arrive at meaning but in the sense of defining what it means to read and write. To be literate, in this view, is to be like a text.

But this post-hoc, text-centered model of literacy disintegrates in the scrutiny of real writers and readers at work. Although studies of writing and reading processes have only really gotten under way in the last couple of decades, they are fairly unanimous in showing that the crucial action in writing and reading goes on in a rich, dynamic mental setting of purpose, memory, inference, anticipation, and insight. Sustaining meaning in writing and reading requires sustaining the process itself—figuring out what actions to take next. And only in relation to the here-and-now work of writing and reading does textual language make sense to human beings.

These realizations about the nature of writing and reading processes allows an important decoupling of literacy from the institution of textuality as well as the possibility of reinterpreting what we think of as essential textualness. As material objects, texts obviously serve archival purposes—and those purposes must be considered part of what texts mean in the culture. But it is equally true, and equally important to the understanding of literacy, that texts are the way they are because they facilitate the work of writing and reading. They are not merely the objects of outcome for writers nor the objects of consumption for readers. They are the means by which present-tense literate acts are carried out. Writers have to know not only how to compose texts but how to use their own texts to compose with. Readers have to know not only how to recognize written words but how to recognize what those words have to do with what they are supposed to be doing. In short, literate acts must proceed with an awareness of the intersubjective undertalk that is carried in written language—undertalk that refers to the work of writing and reading and the people who are involved right here, right now, with that work. This undertalk, which infuses every element of written language, serves to orient writer and reader to the public conditions that are mutually theirs, mutually relevant. Out of these public, concerted conditions—the state of the "we"—writer and reader can carry out their decisions about what to do now.

To understand writing and reading as intersubjective processes and texts as facilitators in those processes is to arrive at a fundamentally different characterization of literacy than the prevailing strong-text accounts provide. Literate knowledge has been seen fundamentally as metalinguistic knowledge—knowledge about language as an opaque and independent system. Acknowledging this system as a separate, stable locus of meaning has been considered the first, necessary step in the transition from orality to literacy. However, a look at writers and readers at work argues strongly for the case that literate knowledge is fundamentally metacommunicative knowledge—knowledge about how people use written-down language to sustain ad hoc involvement in order to arrive at meaning. In the prevailing view, the challenge of becoming literate is learning to fall under the powers of language on its own, to make meaning in the absence of social relationships and social action, to detach oneself in order to deal with abstract language. However, in reality, such language-centeredness and psychic separation in reading and writing usually lead to breakdowns in meaning and disruption of the very acts themselves. Effective writers and readers at work see contextual reference in written language. They see how a text relates dynamically and immediately to people, place, time, and action—even more specifically, to a me, a you, a here, and a now. *How it relates* is the real challenge in literacy learning—indeed, that is the continual interpretive challenge of any act of reading or writing.[3]

In strong-text analyses, written language is message rich and involvement poor. Intersubjective background recedes in formal written exchanges, according to these theories, as ideational content fills the spaces of importance and as the exacting capacities of the literate technology make a text self-sufficient and self-referential. But from the "on-line" perspectives of writers and readers in action, the very features that have been considered the hallmarks of autonomous text take on a different significance—indexing a joint writer-reader history and referring outside the text, to the ongoing accomplishments by which writer and reader manage their sense of what is going on here. Rather than being relatively low in what Tannen calls involvement focus, formal written texts verge on utter involvement focus as the engagement of two minds—writer's and reader's—becomes the whole point and basis of exchange. In other words, what have been characteristically treated as the most formal, message-dense, and autonomous texts are actually texts that refer more and more exclusively to the acts of writing and reading that are under way. These texts talk primarily about what writer and reader are in the act of doing here together. What is made explicit in these so-called explicit texts is how writer and reader are accomplishing understanding together. The language of these texts borders on pure metacommunication. And to compose or construe them requires (among other things) long abiding experience with the intersubjective work of writing and reading—pragmatic knowledge about how literate work gets done. Only out of that concrete experience can the abstract words of these kinds of texts make good sense.

Chapter Five

"The Ties of the Moment": Literacy as Involvement

Insights into the metacommunicative foundations of literacy help to resolve the paradox with which this study began, revealing social involvement as not merely a cultural impetus for literacy, but its interpretive underpinning as well. While the move from the oral to the literate does require a new level of symbolic reflectiveness, it does not require a renunciation or reformulation among context, language, and meaning that pertains in oral language use. Rather, it requires a familiarity with the pragmatic work of writing and reading to which literate language refers. Consequently we must see literacy not as a shift of the burden of meaning away from context and onto the formal properties of texts but rather as intensified reflection upon and control over the ways that people use language to sustain the processes of intersubjective life.

There has been a certain willingness (especially in education) to acknowledge literacy as a socially contextualized practice on the large scale while continuing to describe the demands of individual acts of reading and writing—particularly of so-called autonomous, academic exposition—in terms of linguistic, cognitive, and interpersonal decontextualization. In other words, we have tended to regard literacy as a technical capacity that is introduced into various social contexts, acknowledging that literacy and context co-condition each other but seeing the two as separate, either antagonistic or conspiratorial sources of influence. What we have to begin to contemplate is that the "technical" capacity of literacy is of a piece with social contexts and is enabled only by them. That in fact is the implication of recent, multidisciplinary findings about the social roots of literacy, as exemplified in the works of Scribner and Cole; Heath; Bleich; Graff; and others. The present study, by deliberately focusing on individual acts of writing and reading and on the "decontextualized" language of expository essays, has been a start toward a more satisfactory reconciliation of social and cognitive explanations of literacy. Viewing reading and writing as forms of metacommunicative knowledge is more consonant with a view of literacy as pluralistically and culturally constituted.

Articulating that consonance is the general business of this chapter. It will explore implications of the "involvement focus" of literate cognition, especially as they match up with recent research and pedagogical reforms that advocate a social approach to literacy learning. While suggestions here overlap with initiatives already proposed and under way by others, I hope this discussion will further amplify and justify those initiatives.

Of particular interest in this chapter is how an understanding of literacy as involvement compels a reanalysis of the sources of literacy success and failure in school, whether among beginning readers in elementary school or initiates into academic discourse at the college level. If strong-text theories extrapolate from the objectified text to derive conceptions of literate development, this chapter will extrapolate from the social foundations of reading and writing processes to argue why social involvement is the lifeblood of literate development.

To do that it will be necessary to back up and consider why in the first place strong text has been such an appealing model for school-based literacy instruction.

The Influence of Strong Text

As I just mentioned, it has seemed easy to acknowledge the pluralistic, context-dependent nature of literacy in the real world while proceeding to teach reading and writing in school on the model of the neutral, decontextualized text (C. Gould and K. Gould; Welch). What makes strong-text conceptions of literacy so congenial as a model for reading and writing instruction in school? Chapter One established what David Olson and others regard as the elegant symmetry between oral-literate and home-school contrasts. Removing children from homes and other social affiliations to place them at individual desks facing flat surfaces of chalkboards and texts for instruction and individual assessment physically emulates the interpretive transitions that literacy in the strong-text view is said to embody. Leonard Scinto, in fact, asserts that literacy cannot be conceptually separated from schooling because, in practice, children become literate by dealing with the "scholarized discourse" of the school (69).

As students are intentionally decontextualized from the community, the detached text rises as the new center of attention. In a context shaped solely by the aim to teach reading and writing as ends in themselves, the text as product becomes the standard toward which instruction aims. So, in one sense, strong-text literacy is a practical answer to the physical circumstances of schooling, in which one teacher and twenty-five students are confined to a print-laden room all day.

But the school finds deeper ideological affinities in strong-text models of literacy. As Jenny Cook-Gumperz explains in a marvelously insightful essay on literacy and schooling in the United States and England, the twentieth century has seen the institution of the school utterly take over responsibility for the cognitive development of individuals and their preparation for the labor force. Contrasting contemporary mass schooling with the indigenous, diversified literacy and learning practices of the eighteenth and nineteenth centuries, Cook-Gumperz observes:

> Modern schooling has made school-based learning into a universal and standardised technical skill. In a schooled society individuals undergo a transformation through learning, by virtue of which they become members of the wider society. Educational curricula are a matter of societal decisions so that knowledge is now public not personal or oriented towards a specific or bounded social group. (34)

We see in this defintion of education many of the key elements in strong-text literacy, from an emphasis on literacy as a transformative technology to its demand for a repudiation of immediate social involvement as a basis for knowledge and meaning. Strong-text accounts of literacy and literate ability answer the call of mass schooling, offering just the kind of technological rationale needed for this technological undertaking.

Text-centered models of literacy also reinforce another important component in the ideology of mass education, namely equal, democratic access to literacy. If the potential of literacy abides in texts—if texts carry both the technological orientation and the substantive knowledge that constitute literacy—then the opportunity for equal literacy achievement lies in exposing students equally to texts. This idea, in fact, is behind what E. D. Hirsch, Jr., regards as the essentially democratic spirit of his text-centered cultural literacy project and Jonathan Kozol's recent proposal to flood poor communities with reading materials.[1] Inexpensive, prolific, accessibile, and standard, texts as the bearers of literacy are an indispensable symbol in the dream of modern educational and economic progress.[2]

The entrenchment of school-based literacy, on the one hand, and the recognition of the plurality of real-world literacies on the other intertwine in so-called match-mismatch theories of school success and failure. In match-mismatch formulations, students are deemed to be at risk in school literacy performance to the extent to which their home language is at odds with the so-called explicit, decontextualized language of the school. James Collins and Sarah Michaels describe the problem this way:

> In learning to become literate in school the child has to learn to shift from his or her home-based conversational discourse strategies, which depend on multi-level linguistic inference, to the more discursive strategies preparatory to written expository prose. To the extent that the home-based discourse strategies differ from those of the school, it is this transition between speech and writing which makes the achievement of literacy more difficult. (207–8)

Conceptions of language mismatches between home and school demonstrate Cook-Gumperz's point about the growing influence of the school in treatments of literacy and its problems. Real-world literacies, rather than being models for school literacy development, are treated instead in terms of how well or unwell they prepare children for the unique demands of school literacy.[3] Cook-Gumperz observes that the modern definition of literacy now includes an ability *to be evaluated* in reading and writing (37–40), reflecting the fact that one's literacy level is gauged by one's performance on standardized tests. Likewise, home languages now tend to be evaluated by the same school standards. Evaluation has spilled out of the province of the classroom into relations between social groups and the school. In some research, for instance, homes in which parents read storybooks to young children are typified as "school-oriented" households because such practices are seen as good preparation for reading success in school.[4] In contemporary society, the school has usurped the very meanings that literacy can have, even in the private relations among parents and children.

Language Socialization and School Performance

Match-mismatch theories of school literacy success have built upon the work of British sociolinguist Basil Bernstein, who, in the 1960s, developed the concepts of "restricted" and "elaborated" codes to explain language orientations favored in the talk of different socioeconomic groups and their connection to achievement and nonachievement in school. Subsequently linguists and educators have looked to language socialization as an explanation for why poor and minority students as a group consistently test below middle-class white students in reading and writing achievement at virtually all grade levels.[5] Bernstein argues that students from working-class families in England rely primarily on "restricted" language forms, which he describes as elliptical, context-dependent, concrete, and conformist, expressing or implying shared, communal values. Students from middle-class families, on the other hand, more readily use "elaborated" language forms, which Bernstein describes as relatively explicit, differentiated, decontextualized, and individualistic. Although not offered as a strict and limiting dichotomy (members of both social groups could use both codes under certain circumstances), Bernstein's framework does suggest that preference for one code over the other can be traced to the traditions, values, and language habits of one's social group—all of which are conveyed overtly in child-rearing and language-teaching as well as in the broader power relationships and world views held within families and groups. The school, a middle-class, majority-run institution which is symbol-intensive by nature, relies heavily upon and demands elaborated language forms. Middle-class students are therefore at an immediate advantage upon entering school while working-class students are usually at a disadvantage.

Although Bernstein dealt only with oral language and confined his research to England, his ideas have had resonance for researchers of language patterns among different classes and races in the United States. Some observers, including Hirsch in *Cultural Literacy,* have noted parallels between the "elaborated" oral code and the literate or print code.[6] Plausibly, in social groups whose members read a lot, written forms will be incorporated into oral language. Likewise, there are similarities between Bernstein's characterization of "restricted" codes and prevailing descriptions of orality.

David R. Olson has offered his own version of language codes and school achievement in his explanation of what he calls "literate orientation" (" 'See! Jumping' "). As was mentioned earlier, Olson says that parents in highly literate groups (groups, that is, that rely a good deal on reading) begin to convey to very young children a distinctly literate stance toward language—a stance that treats language as a system that can be separated from the speakers' context and manipulated in its own right. This literate stance is conveyed not merely in overt literacy events like bedtime-story reading but in all sorts of oral exchanges that do not even necessarily involve print. Such cultural coding—which begins long before children actually begin to read and write on their own—prepares them nevertheless, according to Olson, for the fundamental interpretive shift they will need in the move from speaking and listening to reading and writing. This consciousness about language will give them a critical head start in school literacy achievement. To demonstrate this theory, Olson and his colleagues have correlated children's reading success with their use of cognate verbs in conversation, which is taken as a clue that these children are mentally manipulating alternative possibilities— the mark, according to Olson and others, of literate orientation (see Torrance and Olson). Olson treats literate-culture coding somewhat more narrowly than Bernstein, presenting it less as a world view and more as a technical, language-specific orientation whose aim is primarily to encourage reading success.

Research on language socialization and school literacy performance has made several important contributions. Above all it challenges "deficit" theories of literacy failures in schools. Rather than branding students from working classes or racial minorities as "impoverished" language users, such research focuses instead on the clash in language values and functions between home and school, shifting the metaphor from deficit to mismatch. This research also illuminates how the school perpetuates class dominance by virtually tuning out all but the mainstream frequency in classroom discourse. And it points up the complex and difficult social problems that underlie the disparities in literacy achievement, the interdependence of the need for school reform and social change.

As useful and astute as this work has been, however, it has some disturbing ramifications. Although this perspective offers a corrective to blatant deficit explanations of language problems, it still implies that orality or "oral orientation" is an impediment to literacy achievement in school. Children raised in social groups that esteem oral traditions are seen, from this perspective, to be linguistically programmed in an antiliterate way. Thus, they may enter school not simply unfamiliar with book reading but with a stance toward language that allegedly resists the written language code. Instead of a language-deficit theory, we get a kind of language-surplus theory: too much of the wrong kind of language experience.

When the causes of literacy failures are posited so deeply and distantly in cultural arrangements, it is too easy for the school to exempt itself from blame for students' reading difficulties. Disparity in school performance begins to look inevitable; resignation and acceptance too attractive. Other problems creep in as well. Match-mismatch approaches encourage us to think about family language and literacy in terms of how they prepare or do not prepare children for school (rather than considering, for instance, how well the school helps children to function at home). Further, such thinking leads to the injustice alluded to in the introduction: while white, middle-class children sustain themselves in their transition to school by clinging to language customs of family and community, this same process for others is called context-dependence, the dangerous source of certain failure.

These sorts of analyses presume an underlying antagonism between the oral and the literate code. Like the trompe l'oeil figures in psychology experiments that force one to see a wine goblet or a profile but not both, the oral-literate contrast or continuum or seesaw suggests that one orientation will crowd out the other—as one ascends the other must subside; an allegiance to one requires estrangement from the other. Even models that allow for seeing the two in one consider the two in tension with each other. Orality is what is not literacy, and literacy is what is not orality.

Most troubling of all, analyses premised on antagonism between an oral and literate code create exclusionary definitions of standard literacy largely by dint of semantic fiat. To call standard literacy abstract, decontextualized, and psychically separating excludes from its character that which is concrete, contextualized, and communal. Then, to associate certain social groups with loyalty to concrete, contextualized, and communal language is to put them outside the sphere of literate possiblities. But what if, as this discussion has been advocating, standard literacy were recharacterized as concrete, contextualized, and communal? Then adherence to these values would be understood as part of the foundation for literacy.

I am not trying to suggest that all we need to do to solve literacy problems is to call literacy something else. But I do think that if we are going to solve those problems it will help to start calling literacy something else—something more realistic and less disenfranchising. To do that requires, above all, getting literacy off the seesaw with orality, decoupling literacy from an equivalance with textuality, and reclaiming social involvement as the basis of literate experience and literate knowledge.

Literacy as Activity

Match-mismatch explanations of language socialization and school performance not only assume antagonism between oral and literate meaning-making. They also focus narrowly on orientation to language as the key factor in literacy success in school. Thus some researchers of middle-class home life comb parent-child reading episodes for evidence of school-like talk, looking for teacherish questions or "decontextualizing" language strategies that would account for why those children have an easier time of things when they make the transition from home to school.[7] The context of the human relationship of parent and child, the spontaneous meanings and pleasures of reading or other literacy activities are downplayed in a rush to uncover a particular language tic (like a tendency to treat language objectively) that is held up as the crucial precipitator of literate consciousness. In other words, the context of home literacy is seen as significant only to the extent to which it sustains an objectified stance toward language. This line of thinking can lead readily to the conclusion that what children from non-book-reading homes need most when they get to school is crash training in objectifying language. Practice in everything from letter recognition to root and stem words, to spelling, homonyms, and parts of speech, to syllogistic word puzzles testify to the narrow language focus that marks much early language instruction in school (and continues to dominate in traditional remedial classrooms).

The fact is that in virtually all homes children of all socioeconomic backgrounds learn to participate in the language customs of their social group and use language for a wide variety of practical and expressive purposes. Where language customs include reading and writing, pre-school children acquire written language in the same way as oral language, through functional participation in "literacy events" that are significant to their immediate social group. Where social customs specifically include book reading (and not just the "environmental print" on labels, products, signs, and television), children acquire knowledge of textuality in the very same way, through repeated invitations to participate with others in a socially significant event.[8]

In a fifteen-year longitudinal study of thirty-two children from poor and middle-class families in Bristol, England, Gordon Wells recorded the children's earliest verbal interactions with their families and then followed their subsequent achievement through the elementary grades. Wells found no clear-cut differences in oral language development and experience between children of middle- and low-income families. Poor children came to school as enriched in oral language as their affluent counterparts. Class background was, however, associated with children's knowledge about literacy, and knowledge about literacy at the time of entry to school was powerfully linked to subsequent school success. While this study could be read as yet more confirmation of language mismatch between poor children and the school, we might consider instead the match that exists between the two socioeconomic groups in that both successfully initiate their young into various and complex language practices relevant to them. Seeing literacy as the great divide separating the affluent and the poor obscures the fact that both groups provide environments that promote and sustain language learning among all of their children. What should be interesting, then, is not what homes are doing or not doing to match the school but what schools can be doing to match the home.[9]

In arguing for more homelike approaches in school literacy learning, I am not really advocating that the forms and functions of school language be identical to children's home language. But the conditions of literacy learning in school—especially those involving human relationships—should be equivalent to the conditions under which all children successfully master language at home. We have attributed an awfully lot of literacy failure in school to differences in dialect or "clashes" between restricted and elaborated codes—that is, we focus on language forms—rather than inquiring into the basic social processes by which students acquire and sustain the language they have, processes that need to be in place for them to keep on learning new forms of language. That a student uses a particular dialect or language code should never be seen as an impediment to literacy but rather as proof that the student is a language learner in good standing![10]

Thanks to excellent recent research on "emergent" (preschool or home) literacy, parallels can be drawn between oral and written language acquisition, parallels that offer important directions for school literacy reform. Although I cannot provide an exhaustive survey here,[11] I do want to touch on some general outlines that have particular pertinence to our earlier investigation of the cognitive processes of reading and writing. First, young children learn about reading and writing not as aims in themselves but as instruments for other aims. For them, the meanings of print begin with the uses of print. Second, children's explorations of the functions of print go on simultaneously with their growing understanding of and participation in the social activities with which print is associated. Denny Taylor in *Family Literacy* writes that, "Children learn to organize their environment through the use of print. The focus of their attention is not the print per se, but the social organization of their everyday lives. Print is one means of accomplishing this. . . . [C]hildren learn of the multiplicity of literate activities as they learn of different social practices" (52). And she observes, "The children, as integral members of the social organization [of the family], use print as one medium through which they can master their surroundings. It enables them to build new social connections as well as to establish new environmental relationships" (26). Literacy events, as Anderson and Stokes say, are "socially assembled transactions" (28). This stress on the functionality of written language and its systematic, semiotic relationship to a child's social context is exactly what investigators of oral language acquisition find so fundamental to children's learning how to talk (Bates, *Language and Context;* Halliday, *Explorations in the Functions of Language*).

Another major emphasis in emergent literacy research is on children's relationships with literate adults and siblings as the impetus for literacy growth. Observing reading development in a group of children from print-reliant households, Marilyn Cochran-Smith comments, "These preschoolers were not so much surrounded with print as they were surrounded by people who chose to use print because it was effective in many aspects of their everyday life" (92–93). In a similar study of writing development, Robert Gundlach et al. concur: "The people in a child's life and not merely the print in the child's environment constitute the child's chief resource in learning the early lessons of writing. People . . . provide the child with reasons to write, technical and emotional support (or challenge) during the process, and response once the writing is done" (53).

Cochran-Smith also documents the extraordinary range of informal information that passes between adults and children during reading.[12] Adults constantly share information about the functions of stories, concepts of genre, attitudes toward reading, and so on. Especially important, she found, were the ways adults help children elaborate and infer beyond the very words of a text. They help children to identify and use background experience that is relevant to a text and to formulate intellectual and esthetic response to stories. As adults talk around a text, they lead children to figure out what they already know about the world that will help make sense of the text and how to use what they learn from the text to make sense of the world. The focus in reading to children is not on how words are said but on how the process gets managed—the crucial knowledge, as we have seen, that is needed for fluent reading and writing. Cochran-Smith notes of these oral exchanges: "None of these aspects of early literacy is directly related to the processes of encoding or decoding print. . . . Without the knowledge of how to use print, the abilities to encode and decode print are meaningless" (258).

While Cochran-Smith's study deals mostly with storybook reading with children from middle-class, mostly college-educated American families, the process (if not the specifics of the process) is the same in other social groups and with other reading practices. Shirley Brice Heath, struck by the extent to which talk sustained print in the three diverse communities she studied in the Carolina Piedmont, concluded that, "The extension of literacy within a society depends on opportunities for new literates to participate in redundant, multiple, and reinforcing occasions for oral construction of the shared background needed to interpret written materials" (*Ways with Words* 68–69). People do not read themselves into literacy—they have to be talked into it.

Studies of emergent literacy stress two important points that are most relevant to our discussion so far. First, they show that children's growing control over written language must be concomitant with their growing understanding of social practices that involve written language. It also must be concomitant with their growing participation in those practices. When we think about the cognitive demands of reading and writing discussed in earlier chapters, we see why this growing into context is as important as growing into language because context underwrites the references of written language. Without familiarity with the contexts to which written language refers, one cannot make good sense of the words. Learning that reading and writing are always for something, toward some end, also relates directly to the goal-directed efforts that, as we have seen, fuel the cognitive processes of reading and writing. My point in noting these parallels is to show that children's early attempts to relate print to situated social practices are not merely an initial way in to literacy based on childish (oral) interpretive schemes that will eventually need to be reorganized. Rather they are a set of conditions that must continue to obtain for all readers and writers at any stage or age. If we see literacy as the growing ability to use language to sustain intersubjective processes then we have to see that learning about language is only one half of the enterprise. Experiencing intersubjective processes—learning how to participate in the work of life (especially the work that involves print)—has to be given equal attention as a part of literacy development. What John Wilson observes about learning to talk pertains just as much to learning to read and write. Both involve what he calls "an investment in the corporate background against which language is used" (32). "Children," Wilson goes on to say, "become initiated into the forms of thought by being initiated into the forms of life that generate them" (33).

The second important point in emergent literacy research is the role of other people in initiating the young into the actual work of reading. Reading to young children is usually promoted as a way to instill "the love" of reading. But as the research of Cochran-Smith, Heath, Teale, and others has shown, the talk that goes on around reading teaches something more critical: how to sustain the process of reading, how to figure out what to do now. Adults reading with children show them the relationship between words and action, show them how they, as readers, are being addressed by writers, and how reading involves doing things in your head. It would be wrong to interpret adults' oral improvisations while reading to young children as mere compensations for and concessions to children's lingering dependence on the oral context as their attention lapses back to the physical and interpersonal occasion of the reading itself. It would be wrong to see such talk as a crutch for children in the midst of the transition from the oral to the literate way of interpretation. Talk is not merely a temporary scaffold for young initiates: it continues to be a central means by which people come to public consensus about texts and thus sustain their collective brand of literacy. One need only think of the most literacy-intensive institutions in our society—universities, for instance, or the legal system—to realize that the more an institution produces and depends upon written language, the more talk about written language plays a role in that institution.

It is common for emergent literacy studies to end with a lament about the disparity between the spontaneous ways preschool children begin to learn to read and write and the methods they encounter in formal instruction in school. Ferreiro and Teberosky observe:

> To understand print, preschool children have reasoned intelligently, elaborated good hypotheses about writing systems . . . overcome conflicts, searched for regularities, and continually attached meaning to written texts. But the logical coherence they impose on themselves disappears when faced with what the teacher demands from them. They must worry about perception and motor control instead of the need to understand. They must acquire a series of skills instead of coming to know an object. They must set aside their own linguistic knowledge and capacity for thought until they

discover, at a later point, that it is impossible to comprehend a text without them. (279)

It is also clear why children who enter school with the least knowledge of reading and writing cannot get ahead: because the two most potent ingredients in language learning, namely functional context and close human relationships, recede in favor of what Michael Cole and Peg Griffin call "the analytic strategy that we have associated with alphabetic literacy" (118). They go on: "Observers of the operations of reading instruction in the early grades have commented that children who succeed must come to school with some idea of what adults really mean by 'reading' because they rarely get a glimpse of it in school" (118).[13]

Cole and Griffin concentrate their concern on remedial reading instruction in school, which alarmingly becomes even more atomized and decontextualized as attempts are made to break reading down into increasingly discrete skills. In the following description of remedial reading students we see how diametrically opposite their school-based experience is from the experience of the children Denny Taylor described who were learning in family contexts to use print to mediate and master their surroundings. We also ironically hear an allusion to the legacy of strong-text literacy:

> the children have an incorrect conception of the process of reading; instead of using print to help them mediate future activity, they conform as closely as possible to the precise level of the system that their educational experience encourages them to concentrate on. The very tenacity with which they subordinate themselves to instruction fatallly cuts them off from the insight that reading means comprehending. They become "text-bound," parroting the sounds of letters and words. (119)

When Cole and Griffin go on to advocate that "we should be trying to instantiate a basic *activity* when teaching reading and not get blinded by the basic skills" (127) they return our focus to a process-approach to literacy, to a recognition that learning to read and write is learning to know what to do now. Such knowledge is not "text-bound," in that it is not carried in the language of the text. Rather, it is carried in relationships. This includes relationships to other literates, who can pass on literate "know-how." It also includes relationships to social practices for which texts help to sustain meaning and in which the meanings of texts are sustained.

Literacy as Craft and Literate Cultures as Craft Cultures

Seeing reading and writing in terms of social and cognitive know-how invites new ways of thinking about literacy and literate culture that are strikingly different from prevailing strong-text conceptions. As we have seen in earlier discussions, literacy traditionally has been treated as the means by which people transcend parochial boundaries to take up abstract membership in abstract society. As E. D. Hirsch, Jr., explains it in *Cultural Literacy,* literate culture may be somewhat confined by national borders, language, and history but otherwise it has no known local address. It is associated with no particular place, no particular dialect, no particular social groups, except for those who can forsake commitment to locale, dialect, and clan to cross over to the universal, standard ways of literate culture. To be literate requires imagining into existence a new allegiance to a literate tradition. Unlike speech cultures, in which members rub elbows in the give and take of daily exchange, literate culture does not touch. Members of literate culture may never meet. Being literate grants *the potential* to communicate but not necessarily the need. Indeed, because literate culture is seen primarily as a culture of readers, the bond is not even made in direct communication with others but in the common consumption of certain texts. Literate culture, in Hirsch's view, is a culture engineered by texts, a culture more definable by its texts than by what its people do with them, where, when, how, and why.

Historically, literacy is credited not only with reorganizing knowledge but in reconstituting traditional channels of knowledge. Craft apprenticeship disappeared in the nineteenth century with the spread of literacy and the rise of the school (Eisenstein; Soltow and Stevens; Bohme and Stehr). The ability to read knowledge-bearing texts eliminated the social relationship of craftsman to apprentice, as well as the form of knowledge associated with that relationship: a knowledge embodied in a doing. The responsibility for passing knowledge moved away from hand-to-hand, mouth-to-mouth contact and into the codified written text. Literacy allowed a new form of knowledge: propositional, anonymous, and decontextualized. And literate learning became associated with everything that craft-based learning was not: not contextual, not communal, not practical.

But we see in these descriptions many of the strong-text assumptions illuminated in Chapter One, in which the history and institution of texts is conflated with the history and institution of literacy and in which the ability of literate technology to transform knowledge comes to stand in for literate knowledge itself. What literacy makes possible is taken as a model for what makes literacy possible.

This study has been arguing for a view of literacy that is sustained not in texts but in the know-how of readers and writers at work, people who can carry out the dynamic and ad hoc interpretive acts of writing and reading. Those acts are always accomplished through practical considerations of "Maybe this," "When is enough?" and "What now?" To observe readers and writers in action is to appreciate that literate knowledge *is* a knowledge embodied in a doing, a knowledge in which what is made is not separated from the making of it.

Because literacy is sustained not in texts but in readers and writers, literate culture is, by necessity, pluralistic. It has a local address. If the expert writers in Flower and Hayes' studies have anything in common with the children in emergent literacy studies it is just this: they work out of a local address. As we have just seen, the local address for children is especially important because that is where the people are who will show them what reading and writing are about. If literacy is sustained in talk and in repeated occasions for collective practice, then we have to see that its roots are local and that it is embodied in contemporary relationships to family, neighbors, teachers, and friends. When these relationships are assaulted, broken, or betrayed, so is literacy.[14]

The local address is important not only for children learning to read and write but also for full-fledged literates in action. The most successful readers and writers are grounded in an immediate and particular context of need, which gives purpose and direction to an act of reading or writing. Before skills or even background knowledge, literate people need a place to be literate—a place where they and others are asking the kinds of questions and doing the kinds of work that make reading and writing and text-based knowledge purposeful. To be gathered, text-based knowledge needs readers who have ways and places to gather it, who have ways and reasons for bringing text knowledge into their "lifeworld."

Underestimating the local address will continue to be a problem so long as literacy is seen as an embodiment of the standardized and the

118 Literacy as Involvement

decontextualized and as long as it is perceived in terms of potential skill instead of actual experience. The tendency to see literacy in terms of future use permeates school-based language practices and has probably led more than anything to the forms of skills-oriented literacy instruction and testing that we have. Even Hirsch, who recognizes the contextual nature of reading and writing processes, fails to consider adequately the contexts needed for learning those processes. He too sees literacy as a potential. He operates from a view of what literacy makes possible instead of what makes literacy possible. Hirsch writes, "Only by piling up specific, communally shared information can children learn to participate in complex, cooperative activities with other members of their community" (xv). But if we consider what has to be in place in order to sustain reading and writing, the conditions must be reversed: only by learning to participate in complex, cooperative activities with other members of their community can children pile up specific, communally shared information.

A Note on Writing-Across-the-Curriculum

I have been concentrating on beginning readers and writers and their needs for connections to functional contexts of literacy, but these same conditions and arrangements are needed at all stages of literacy growth, particularly when people are entering new spheres—such as specialized academic disciplines. Recently there have been efforts to address these concerns at the college and university level in this country by introducing into undergraduate education what is called writing-across-the-curriculum or writing-in-the-disciplines. But to what extent has this been a genuine reform in literacy education?

The aim of writing-across-the-curriculum is to encourage more writing in content courses, especially writing that aids in learning, writing, that is, that students use to work out ideas instead of merely delivering up their ideas for evaluation. So, instead of assigning big research papers due at the end of a semester, teachers in all disciplines have been encouraged to assign frequent, shorter, exploratory writing and to incorporate revising and teacher and peer response into the process. The overarching aim in the writing-across-the-curriculum movement is both to encourage more writing and to help students learn the specific discourse conventions of their major disciplines, leading to more effective writing and presumably more satisfying intellectual experiences.[15]

While some schools, notably smaller colleges, have made significant strides in spreading writing (and the responsibility for writing instruction) throughout the curriculum, many more schools, especially larger ones, have incorporated writing-across-the-curriculum approaches into lower-level writing courses housed in English departments or in special composition programs. Textbooks for such courses proliferate, offering introductions to the languages and research methods of the humanities, social sciences, hard sciences, and so on. Anthologies for such courses include pieces of writing and research reports from a variety of disciplines.

The writing-across-the-curriculum movement has been inspired not only by a desire to use writing more fully as a vehicle for learning but also by a growing appreciation of the social nature of written language. Academic disciplines are understood as semidiscrete "discourse communities," which operate according to their own rules, conventions, and paradigms of inquiry, with concomitant vocabularies and discourse genres that reflect and further that inquiry. Texts produced by such discourse communities are now understood as somewhat cryptic indexes to the histories, traditions, values, styles, politics, and general epistemologies that give rise to them. To read or write such texts thus requires specific knowledge and sensitivity to the workings of the discourse community, an ability to cope with what James Boyd White calls the "invisible discourse" of a specialized domain, the body of knowledge, assumptions, and operating procedures left out of the surface of a discourse but necessary for understanding and producing it.[16]

At first look writing-across-the-curriculum seems a healthy literacy reform. Certainly it recognizes the plurality of literacies that are operating even within the single institution of the university. And, at least conceptually, it stresses the relationship between text and context, language and work. Further, it has led to important scholarly and pedagogical research. Charles Bazerman in *Shaping Written Knowledge,* for instance, has rendered a stimulating historical study of the rise—and social functioning—of scientific articles. Patricia Bizzell in "What Happens When Basic Writers Come to College?" has treated the importance of making insider academic conventions accessible to all beginning college students, especially basic writers, while at the same time encouraging students to develop critical stances toward the conventions.

But for all these healthy signs, there remains something troubling about the way that writing-across-the-curriculum is taking shape: around texts. That is, the primary method of teaching the "invisible discourse" of a discipline is by explicitly introducing its textual conventions, examining their presence in various texts, and (sometimes) explaining their relationship to the work of the discipline. The tacit knowledge of a discipline, in other words, is made into explicit propositions and presented to students in textual form. While sensitivity to the discourse community may be an advance over old-fashioned formalist analysis of texts, this is nevertheless a case in which literate learning (gaining explicit propositional knowledge by reading) is standing in for literacy learning (a knowledge acquired by doing).

Such instruction rests on a model that I think is flawed in two ways. First, there is an overemphasis on *discourse* as the constituter of a community. Looking at a community's language can certainly tell us a lot about it. Understanding the language of a social group can be a way in to understanding its life. But understanding language alone cannot be a way in to membership in a social group. Treating "discourse communities" separately from their actual economic, political, and social realities, as though they function only through a common discourse, smacks of the same strong-text assumptions that we encountered earlier.

Second, the writing-across-the-curriculum model assumes that membership in a discourse community awaits those who acquire insider knowledge. Lower-level university students study the texts and conventions of their major disciplines so that they will be prepared for eventual admission. But what I have been arguing—and the message that comes over and over again from literacy research—is that *you have to be a member first to acquire insider knowledge.* "Tacit" knowledge must accumulate tacitly—as an outgrowth of routine participation. What separates the "outlander" basic writers that Bizzell writes about is not their ignorance of academic codes but their long-standing exclusion from academic membership. Membership must be granted—in fact, taken for granted—for literacy learning to proceed. This, of course, requires granting membership status to students (which is, regrettably, not usual in the institution of the school), accepting them as active knowledge users, knowledge makers, and even "paradigm shifters" from the very start. The political power latent in genuine literacy begins not with its acquisition but with the social relationships that are necessary for genuine acquisition to take place.

On the Writing and Reading Workshop

In criticizing what I see as stubbornly text-centered approaches to literacy transmission in school, I do not mean to overlook the many efforts to bring a more contextual, socially oriented emphasis to reading and writing in the classroom. The "whole language" movement in elementary education, which advocates immersing youngsters in reading and writing whole texts rather than focusing on mastery of subskills, certainly puts a premium on functionality and activity as stimulants in written-language learning.[17] Likewise the process movement in writing, which encourages teachers to write along with their apprentice pupils and students to serve as communities of readers for each others' writing, offers the potential for profound change in school-based literacy arrangements, providing these innovations are regarded not merely as progressive methods for teaching reading and writing but as ways to sustain the ongoing conditions that literates need to be literates. What I would like to do here, in fact, is to defend the process-centered workshop from some recent criticisms while addressing some of its current limitations.

By process-centered workshop I mean mostly models first promulgated by the Bay Area Writing Project and by teacher-researchers including Donald Murray, Donald Graves, and Nancie Atwell. Writing workshops generally make students' writing, rather than textbook guides, the center of attention, and class time is given to such practical, process-oriented activities as brainstorming topics, talking over plans, reading drafts aloud, discussing directions for revising, editing for eventual publication, and sharing published writing. Explicit instruction is minimized and teachers serve as advisers and collaborators, allowing students authority to make their own authorial decisions. Correctness in grammar, spelling, and punctuation is managed mainly on an individual, need-to-know basis. Students hold frequent conferences with teachers and each other. The emphasis is on developing students who think and work as real writers.

If literacy is a craft knowledge and literate knowledge is sustained through the word-of-mouth of people who read and write, then the workshop is a potentially critical site for literacy growth. In the workshop, the work of writing is made manifest to all and the teacher as craftsperson, or demonstrator in Frank Smith's sense of the word, is an especially valuable resource for passing on know-how, by writing with students and guiding them, with decreasing interventions, in the production of texts.[18] The sheer demand in the workshop for articulating the usually silent and hidden procedures by which texts are made and changed stands to heighten the reflectiveness by which students can better manage the cognitive processes of writing. The close proximity of readers responding on-the-spot also can emphasize the relationship of written words to intersubjective contexts. All in all the workshop keeps the connection between written language and the work it refers to explicitly and concretely in the foreground.

One could certainly justify a similar workshop approach to classroom reading and, in fact, Nancie Atwell offers such directions in her inspiring *In the Middle: Writing, Reading, and Learning with Adolescents.* Cognitive modeling of reading processes, collaborative reading, as well as ample opportunity to work through interpretations of texts step-by-step (rather than simply using finished interpretations as a basis for discussion) all would emphasize for students the degree to which the meaning of print has to do with what readers are up to when they read. Problems of comprehension, rather than being sources of embarrassment for students, can be occasions for exploring how interpretations are put together and how they can be revised. Exposing the tacit and usually hidden procedures by which people "make" readings—as well as displaying the functional activities that reading is made for—would be the key in reading workshops. Such arrangements also would provide the human support system in school that usually sustains successful readers outside of school. Finally, like Donald Graves' workshops for young writers, such reading workshops would take for granted that all members are readers who, with work and support, can be successful.

Serious weaknesses arise, however, in the scenarios I have just presented, weaknesses that already have been raised by critics of "process." Consider the matter of the larger social meanings of writing, reading, and texts that were discussed in Chapter Two in connection with cognitive-process research and were just raised again in connection with writing-across-the-curriculum. Frequently in a writing workshop *what* a student is writing becomes merely an occasion for firing up the engines of drafting, peer reviewing, and revising. The social origins and nature of the *what*, the text, is treated as an outcome of that process and not in terms of its larger contextual and conventional connections. James Berlin in "Rhetoric and Ideology in the Writing Class" criticizes process or what he calls "cognitive rhetoric" for treating writing as a kind of closed, cybernetic system generated by the individual goals of an individual writer in a context that extends no farther than a writer's immediate rhetorical problem (or, we might say, at best, no farther than the workshop setting). A pedagogy that focuses only on writers' problem-solving, Berlin argues, presents itself as value-neutral and in doing so fails to spark students' critical consciousness about the ideological interests inherent in all language use, including their own. In that way, according to Berlin, such a pedagogy enhances or at least does not disturb the interests of a ruling economic elite.[19]

It is for reasons like these that I think enthusiasm for "process, not product" has been tempered in recent years by more interest in academic discourse structures and their inherent ideologies. This interest seems especially strong at the moment among college-level teachers and especially among those who teach large numbers of the historically dispossessed: working-class students, African-Americans, Hispanics, returning adult women. For these students consciousness of ideological differences is usually easy enough but knowledge of and comfort with the prestige discourse is often elusive. Gaining control over academic language appears a pressing first order of business, and the process-workshop approach can seem a long and possibly precarious way around the block to this essential information.

This criticism grows in legitimacy when we consider that writing workshops have been mostly a white, middle-class phenomenon. Public schools where writing workshops proliferate tend to be in rural or suburban areas with fairly homogeneous, majority populations.[20] The national writing project—a system for disseminating process approaches to writing by engaging teachers themselves in writing workshops—has not been particularly attractive to black educators, according to Lisa D. Delpit. In an essay called "Skills and Other Dilemmas of a Progressive Black Educator" Delpit writes of her experience as a teacher using a process orientation in a multiracial school in Philadelphia. She found that some of the sacred tenets of the process approach failed to meet the needs of her black students. Delpit suggests that the process pedagogy has been weakened by the absence of black perspectives. Her essay seems to say that the "meaningful contexts" advocated so heartily in the philosophies of whole language and process pedagogy can only be meaningful to the extent to which all participants have certain "skills," which she defines as "useful and useable knowledge which contributes to a student's ability to communicate effectively in standard, generally acceptable literary forms" (384).[21]

It is beyond the bounds of this discussion to treat the broad and recurrent tensions that Delpit raises and nearly all teachers face, no matter what their methods, in balancing care for students' existing ways of thinking, speaking, and writing with the need to show them other, more "generally acceptable" ways. What I do want to plead, though, is that a focus on the work and working out of writing and reading by individuals—the focus in the literacy workshop—does not have to have the limitations just described, providing that "writing" and "reading" are recognized in their cultural plurality and that that plurality is recognized as part of the interpretive problem that writers and readers always face. As pressing as it is to help historically excluded students win the keys to academic and economic achievement by learning "standard" literacy, that goal does nothing toward broadening the base of the "standard" itself—a change that is necessary to realize genuinely pluralistic institutions and a pluralistic democracy. If "standard" literacy is to be achieved among all students, then the scope of the "standard" must broaden. If standard skills are to be achieved by all, then what counts as standard skills also has to broaden. Pluralism not only requires that many voices be heard but that the differences in those voices be understood. Thus, it is not enough to say that everyone is welcome in the "big tent" of literate culture[22] without acknowledging that they will be bringing new materials with which to remake the tent. The literacy workshop—which makes collective processes of interpretation the conscious center of study—can be a unique place for this transformation to be realized. Language "clashes"—rather than being called the source of literacy failure—can be made into the catalyst for sharpening everyone's literacy.

Conclusion: Literacy as Involvement

In a wonderful essay on meaning and language, the ethnographer Bronislaw Malinowski describes a group of Trobriand Islanders working together to capture a shoal of fish in their nets. Listening to their talk, Malinowski is struck by how much the meaning of their utterances is embedded in the unfolding event, driven by what he calls "the ties of the moment without which unified social action is impossible" ("The Problem of Meaning" 310). He writes: "Each utterance is essentially bound up with the context of situation and with the aim of pursuit. . . . The vocabulary, the meaning of the particular words used in their characteristic technicality, is not less subordinate to action" (311).

In the traditional view, of course, this scene epitomizes the state of orality or preliteracy: situation bound, practical, concrete, communal, and action oriented.[23] These qualities of both scene and language are, in the prevailing view, what must be transformed or revoked in the conversion to literacy—as literates must emulate the escape of the abstract written word from dependence on the here-and-now and the with-you. Compared to the talk of bending, calling fishermen, scanning the waters of a coral lagoon, a text appears out of place and time, alienated from human action, an object to be stared at in silence.

I have been arguing throughout this discussion, however, for a reinterpretation of the scene Malinowski describes, not as an antithesis of literacy but as a model for it and a key for reapproaching some of our most vexing and urgent literacy problems. Writers and readers at work, especially those who know what they are doing, are immersed in practical contexts of action, in which the important interpretive decisions are always toward determining what to do now. The aim is to keep the process itself viable, to keep making one's own decisions make sense, and to figure out what to do when they do not.

Writers and readers (again, especially the effective ones) are able to carry out this interpretive work because when they look at written language they see what it is saying, right here, right now, about what they should (or could) be doing. They see how a text is relating to them, as a human presence on the scene. As the processes of writing and reading unfold, writers and readers "meta"-communicate through the undertalk of texts about how the mutual work is proceeding, about how understanding is getting accomplished, and how those accomplishments are aiding in further accomplishments of understanding. A text is a public record of the "unified social action" of writing and reading, a record of a thickening history of involvement that sustains both writer and reader in their efforts after meaning.

Moving from the oral to the literate thus does not require embracing a different interpretation of language, context, and meaning. Like the talk of the Trobriand fishermen, textual language is always embedded in working contexts of action, driven by the "aim of pursuit," its meaning accessible only in reference to the intersubjective enterprises of those who are involved here. Social involvement is at the center both of our collective literate practices and our seemingly solitary efforts at reading and writing.

The history of literacy has been largely and by necessity a history of technology and texts, for acts of reading and writing in themselves leave no such tangible trace. We have come to understand literacy through the evolution of alphabets, the development of print, the production and distribution of books, the records of signatures on wills or church registers or school enrollments.[24] Likewise, we count valued texts as the heritage of literacy, as the major means by which literate knowledge and values are preserved and passed on. It is easy, given the way this history comes to us, to grant a certain autonomy and transcendent power to textual tradition.

But alongside the textual tradition must be recognized the generative social contexts in which reading and writing are practiced as part of everyday life, the contributions made by the hands that turn the pages. Reading and writing survive because they are embedded in so many diverse social practices, nurtured in talk, and valued as instrumental to various ends, individual and collective, which give them point and basis for renewal. Much credit is given, and rightly so, to the powers of written language and the existence of texts as aids in the growth of thinking and knowledge. Written language is the platform for leaps in complex thought.[25] But such leaps are motivated by readers who are able to reinvent the meaning of texts through the new and pressing questions that they pose out of the conditions in which they live and work. They reinvent the meaning of texts out of their ties of the moment. It it these conditions, these questions, and these ties that must be seen as the real preservers of literate knowledge.

Most central of all are the human ties to other readers and writers for they have the knowledge of the craft of literacy, a knowledge that must be preserved and passed hand-to-hand, mouth-to-mouth, in acts of writing and reading with each other. That is why, to be literate, you have to be aboard the boat. You have to see how to pull the nets.

Notes

Works Cited

Index

Notes

Introduction

1. Goody's first formulations of the role of written language in precipitating syllogistic reasoning appears in his 1968 essay with Ian Watt, "The Consequences of Literacy." For Goody's revised views see *The Interface Between the Written and the Oral*, particularly chapter 11.

2. For Tannen's early formulations of "oral-like" and "literate-like" aspects of discourse, see "The Oral-Literate Continuum." Her later conceptualizations appear in "Relative Focus on Involvement."

3. For treatment of the relationship between social cognition and writing ability, see works by Donald L. Rubin.

4. Brazilian educator Paulo Freire has been the leading theorist of a "critical" literacy geared to the emancipation of peasants and other oppressed people. Reading and writing that are truly literate, according to Freire, must always proceed with an awareness of the ideological interests embodied in words. See his *Pedagogy of the Oppressed* and the more recent *Literacy: Reading the Word and the World*, coauthored with Donaldo Macedo.

Chapter 1: Strong Text: Opacity, Autonomy, and Anonymity

1. For useful overviews of the major orality-literacy issues, see Andee Rubin; also Akinasso. For linguistic differences, see works by Chafe. For arguments for the cognitive consequences of literacy, see Greenfield; Luria; also D'Angelo's "Luria on Literacy." For a revisionist perspective on cognitive consequences, see Scribner and Cole. Treatments of orality-literacy-schooling are provided by Scinto; also see Collins and Michaels; Cook-Gumperz.

2. For an interesting alternative to the stereotype of solitary reading, consider Heath's report in *Ways with Words* about Trackton, a black, working-class community in the Carolina Piedmont, where reading among adults is done collectively in public areas. As one person reads

aloud, the group interprets a text together. For another endorsement of the Ongian perspective, see Havelock.

3. For a discussion of the linguistics of strong text, see Ong, *Orality and Literacy,* especially pp. 101–8.

4. See also Kathleen Gough, "Implications of Literacy in Traditional China and India."

5. This criticism can be traced back to Goody and Watt's "The Consequences of Literacy," an essay that Goody later said would have been better titled "The Implications of Literacy," so as not to imply inevitable and unique cognitive consequences of written language. For a discussion of Goody's change in thinking (and an argument that, perhaps, his views have not changed all that much), see Walters.

6. For an extended treatment of Kjolseth's views, see my "Toward an Understanding of Context in Composition."

7. Derrida radically alters the orality-literacy contrast by arguing that all language is written. He maintains that the intersubjective "absences" and "gaps" generally perceived in literate language are, in fact, the condition for all forms of language, including speech. This study argues for the dense intersubjective "presence" in all language—not just in speech but in writing.

Chapter 2: "What Now?": The Processes of Involvement

1. For useful overviews of the process influence in composition teaching and research, see Faigley et al., especially chapter 1. Also see Hairston; Freedman et al.

2. For additional perspectives on oral protocols as a method for investigating writing, see Dobrin; also Flower and Hayes, "Response" to Cooper and Holzman.

3. For an early, linear model of composing see Rohman. Also see Emig, *Composing Processes* for one of the first conceptual revisions to linear models of composing.

4. For a blueprint of what a process-sensitive assessment might be like, see Faigley et al.

5. Flower and Hayes refer to a writer's "rhetorical problem" or "rhetorical situation" (see "Cognition of Discovery" and "A Cognitive Process Theory"). According to Flower and Hayes, writers, as they compose, develop and maintain a mental representation that includes (but is not

limited to) a representation of the emerging text. This mental representation guides a writer's decision-making process. For a process-sensitive theory of literacy, we will need to understand better the origins of writers' (and readers') representations for it is likely that they are an important factor in literate "ability" or "orientation."

6. See, for instance, Winograd; McGee; Paris and Myers; Vipond and Hunt ("Point Driven"). Also see Fisher and Peters.

7. I first heard the word "strategic" used emphatically in connection with composing processes by Linda Flower in a paper, "Entering Academic Discourse: The Power of Novice Strategies," presented at the 1987 Conference on College Composition and Communication in Atlanta, Georgia.

8. The data reported here is taken from a larger study (Brandt, "Writer, Context, and Text") involving some twenty-five hours of protocols by two writers as they drafted and edited six essays in conjunction with an introductory composition course in which they were enrolled in the summer of 1983.

9. This writer began all his writing episodes by looking in Bartlett's for entries that in some way related to his paper topic. Then he would put the relevant quote at the top of his paper. Sometimes the quote would survive to the final draft but just as often it would drop out by the time the paper was ready for submission.

10. I am indebted here especially to Shanklin's groundbreaking work.

11. The assignments were an analytical report, an argument, and an interview. For further descriptions of the contexts of these tasks and explanations of the methodology, see Brandt, "Writer, Context, and Text." For follow-up linguistic analysis of these texts, see Brandt, "Text and Context."

12. Although revising and editing obviously can serve quite different functions and involve different concerns, the frequency with which they occurred in these protocols did not warrant trying to make a distinction. Revision and editing became more pronounced in later writing cycles, after the students had gotten down rough drafts.

Chapter 3: The Language of Involvement

1. Many oral-protocol (i.e., think-aloud) studies of writers and readers reveal a kind of subtextual bantering that goes on, especially by expert writers and readers. They construct an idea of their interlocutor, assigning motives and intentions to this other person that become part

of the interpretive basis from which writer or reader works. On the writer side, see Flower and Hayes' "The Cognition of Discovery." On the reading side, see two works by Vipond and Hunt; also Kintgen; Haas and Flower.

2. Given-new, sometimes referred to as old-new, refers to the distribution of information across a text or a sentence in a way that accommodates the assumed knowledge-state of the reader. Given information is that which a reader already is assumed to know or believe, while the new is the "news." Usually, given information precedes new information. The best introduction to given-new concepts is by Ellen Prince. Also see Vande Kopple ("Given and New") and Witte for excellent discussions of communicative dynamism. Theme-rheme is a related concept, having more to do with what is in current shared focus, what a discourse or sentence is about (theme) and what is being said about it (rheme). Halliday calls theme a "point of departure" for an utterance and aligns it with the first syntactic unit of a sentence ("Notes on Transitivity and Theme").

3. For more on metadiscourse, see Gerald Prince; also Crismore.

4. See Suleiman and Crosman, and for useful comparisons of reader-response theories, Mailloux. Wolfgang Iser writes, "The real reader is always offered a particular role to play, and it is this role that constitutes the concept of the implied reader" (*Act of Reading* 34). Jonathan Culler describes the "ideal reader" as "a theoretical construct perhaps best thought of as a representation of the central notion of acceptability" (123–24), which falls along the lines of Eco's "model reader." For other formulations, see Bruce.

5. See Iser's "Texts and Readers."

6. Flower talks about the unpredictable variation in writers' uses of text formats, information sources, and strategies and goals in "The Role of Task Representation in Reading to Write." This study also describes how writers can proceed from a sense of "local event" or "lucky event" (17), rather than from a large, integrated overview of the task. For a treatment of "current meaning," see Flower and Hayes' "Images, Plans, and Prose."

7. For Ong's treatment of this phenomenon, see "The Writer's Audience," especially pp. 12–15. Also see Rommetveit for his discussion of "proleptic" (pp. 87–88). Rommetveit observes:

> What from an externally imposed or "public" point of view may be considered erroneous presuppositions on the part of the

speaker may hence often more appropriately be conceived of as *self-fulfilling assumptions by which the listener is made an insider of a tacitly expanded shared here-and-now.* He is made an insider precisely because that expanded social reality is taken for granted rather than explicitly spelled out. This is not only the case in everyday conversations ... but also in human discourse of an ideological or even presumably scientific nature. What is said serves on such occasions to induce presuppositions and trigger anticipatory comprehension, and what is made known will hence necessarily transcend what is said. (88)

8. For theoretical foundations of inner speech, see Vygotsky; Piaget; and Luria (*Cognitive Development; Language and Cognition*). For discussions of the relevance of inner speech to writing see Moffett; also Flower's "Writer-Based Prose."

9. I have removed two subheads from the text, one at the beginning called "The NWP Model" and another, "Effects on Teacher Attitude," that appears after the second paragraph.

Chapter 4: Rhetorics of Involvement

1. The quotation marks around "beat-up" present an interesting interpretive dilemma. Do the marks belong to Carter or to us?

2. See, for instance, D'Angelo's "Paradigms as Structural Counterparts of *Topoi.*"

3. For a brilliant explanation of the semiotic basis of emergent reading and writing, see Harste, Burke, and Woodward.

Chapter 5: "The Ties of the Moment": Literacy as Involvement

1. In *Cultural Literacy,* Hirsch writes: "Historically, the modern democratic nations arose at the same time as the great national literate languages, and, ever since, democracy and literate culture have been esssentially connected" (106). From Kozol: "What if it were possible somehow to flood the nation—from the smallest villages of northern Maine and southern Arizona to the mining neighborhoods of Appalachia and the streets of the South Bronx and Boston and Seattle—with three or four hundred million free and excellent and brand-new books? What if we

did this, not just once, but month after month, year after year, for ten or twenty years?" (149).

2. Of course, democratic access to public education proceeds along *stratified* class lines. Schooling is offered to all, but the kind of schooling one gets will be influenced by economic, ethnic, racial, and gender factors. For a useful historical overview of the stratified public school, see Cook-Gumperz.

3. For refreshing, non-school-centered approaches to children's language, see Wells and anything ever written by Dyson.

4. See, for instance, Schieffelin and Cochran-Smith, p. 4.

5. For an explanation of Bernstein's "restricted" and "elaborated" codes, see *Class, Codes, and Control,* vol. 1, epecially chapter 9. Irwin S. Kirsch and Ann Jungeblut, in their profiles of literacy among young American adults, report national reading proficiencies for grades 4, 8, and 11, all of which show a *widening gap* in reading performance between white and black students as a group as they progress through the grades (40). Kirsch and Jungeblut do report, though, that "there is some recent evidence that proficiencies of minority students are increasing at a faster rate than those of their white majority peers" (41). For troubling statistics on the writing side, see Applebee, Langer, and Mullis, p. 45.

6. Hirsch, *Cultural Literacy,* p. 69. For a pretty scathing critique of the use Hirsch makes of Bernstein, see "Three Views," Scholes' review of *Cultural Literacy.* Then, for follow-up commentary, see Hirsch's "Comments on *Profession 88*" and a reply by Scholes.

7. See, especially, Snow; also Olson's " 'See! Jumping!' " Heath also has written of what she sees as critical factors in literacy development, including, she says, an ability to recognize language "as such" ("Critical Factors"). For somewhat different treatments, see Cochran-Smith; Taylor; and Leichter.

8. Particularly fascinating studies in this area include Harste, Burke, and Woodward; Bissex; Ferreiro and Teberosky; and Goodman. Goodman found widespread, equal ability to read "environmental print" among preschoolers across all socioeconomic groups. Some 60 percent of three-year-olds and 80 percent of four- and five-year-olds can read such things as labels on toothpaste cartons or logos from fast-food restaurants.

9. It is traditionally held, of course, that the capacity for speech is innate and thus develops naturally, while literacy requires direct intervention and enculturation. Kieran Egan points out how much cultural,

social, and interpersonal support exists for encouraging and sustaining speech development and wonders provocatively what literacy might be possible if the cultural supports for reading and writing were as ubiquitous.

10. Vivian Horner minimizes language dialect, either as an interference or as a catalyst for reading, and focuses instead on the basic intersubjective awareness that reading requires. She writes:

> I would also argue that the important thing for a child to understand is not that this is *my* speech written down (though it is very important in writing), but rather that this is somebody talking to me. If I can manage to decipher aloud, following those little black squiggles on the paper, and say something, whether it sounds like what I say or whether it sounds like what somebody else says, then I'm still going to be very interested in reading, because that's the way that I listen to somebody who's not there. (139)

11. For a useful survey of this burgeoning area of research, see William H. Teale and Elizabeth Sulzby's introduction to *Emergent Literacy,* "Emergent Literacy as a Perspective for Examining How Young Children Become Writers and Readers."

12. Also see Teale's "Reading to Young Children" and "Toward a Theory of How Children Learn to Read and Write Naturally."

13. Also see MacGinite and MacGinite on this issue.

14. R. P. McDermott writes of the extent to which classroom relationships among students and teachers are absolutely critical to literacy learning. Teachers and students must, he says, have "'working agreements' or 'consensus' . . . about who they are and what is going on between them, agreements which they formulate, act upon, and use together to make sense of each other" (199). He goes on to assert that "successful acquisition of literacy, like the successful use of a pedagogical style, depends on the achievement of trusting relations" (288). What McDermott seems to be saying is that teaching students to read and write requires modeling, as a teacher, the relationships that obtain between writers and readers. Also see Cummins.

15. For background on writing-across-the-curriculum, see Fulwiler; Fulwiler and Young; Hamilton; and Knoblauch and Brannon. For what I see as the "discourse" bias in models of disciplinary learning, see Bartholomae; Maimon; Perelman; and Bazerman ("What Written Knowledge Does"). More recent treatments of writing-across-the-curriculum

issues include Griffin, and Herrington. Examples of textbooks for lower-level introductions to writing-across-the-curriculum are Maimon et al. and Comley et al.

16. White argues that it is not the vocabularly or sentence structure that makes legal discourse impenetrable to outsiders but rather the systematic and procedural constraints at work in the legal context, what he calls the "cultural syntax" of a specialized discourse.

17. See Newman; also Hunt's "A Horse Named Hans."

18. For starters on cognitive modeling of writing (and, potentially, reading), see Bereiter and Scardamalia.

19. Although more sympathetic to "expressionist rhetoric" than to "cognitive rhetoric," for its subversive possibilities, Berlin also faults expressionist pedagogy for focusing on the individual independent of social and economic contexts.

20. Testimonies have mainly come so far from New Hampshire, Maine, and suburban school districts in Massachusetts and California.

21. For a hopeful report on writing workshops in a multiracial, urban school, see Goldblatt.

22. This is an illusion to Hirsch, (*Cultural Literacy*, p. 103).

23. Malinowski himself originally maintained a distinction between context-bound primitive language and abstract scientific language. But he later retracted that view, acknowledging the radically pragmatic nature of all language. See *Coral Gardens and Their Magic*, vol. 2, especially part four.

24. For thoughtful discussions of the methods of historical reconstruction of literacy see Cressy, especially chapter 3, and the opening chapter of Lockeridge.

25. I am indebted to Professor Yi Fu Tuan for the image of writing as a platform of thought in a talk he gave at the University of Wisconsin–Madison in the summer of 1984.

Works Cited

Akinasso, F. Niyi. "The Consequences of Literacy in Pragmatic and Theo-retical Perspectives." *Anthropology and Educational Quarterly* 12 (1982): 163–200.

Anderson, Alonzo B., and Shelley J. Stokes. "Social and Institutional Influences on the Development and Practice of Literacy." *Awakening to Literacy.* Eds. Hillel Goelman, Antoinette Oberg, and Frank Smith. Exeter, NH: Heinemann Educational Books, 1984. 24–37.

Applebee, Arthur N. *Writing in the Secondary School.* Urbana: National Council of Teachers of English, 1981.

Applebee, Arthur N., Judith A. Langer, and Ina V. S. Mullis. *The Writing Report Card: Writing Achievement in American Schools.* Princeton: Educational Testing Service, 1986.

Atwell, Margaret. "The Evolution of Text: The Interrelationship of Read-ing and Writing in the Composing Process." Ph.D. diss., Indiana Univ., 1980.

Atwell, Nancie. *In the Middle: Writing, Reading, and Learning with Adolescents.* Portsmouth, NH: Boynton/Cook, 1987.

Augustine, Dorothy, and W. Ross Winterowd. "Speech Acts and the Reader-Writer Transaction." *Convergences: Transactions in Reading and Writing.* Ed. Bruce T. Petersen. Urbana: National Council of Teach-ers of English, 1986. 127–48.

Bar-Hillel, Yehosua. "Indexical Expressions." *Mind* 63 (1954): 359–79.

Bartholomae, David. "Inventing the University." *When a Writer Can't Write.* Ed. Mike Rose. New York: Guilford Press, 1986.

Bates, Elizabeth. *The Emergence of Symbols: Cognition and Communi-cation in Infancy.* New York: Academic Press, 1979.

———. *Language and Context: The Acquisition of Pragmatics.* New York: Academic Press, 1976.

Bazerman, Charles. *Shaping Written Knowledge: The Genre and Activity of the Experimental Article in Science.* Madison: Univ. of Wisconsin Press, 1988.

———. "What Written Knowledge Does: Three Examples of Academic Prose." *Philosophy of the Social Sciences* 11 (1981): 228–44.

Bereiter, Carl, and Marlene Scardamalia. "From Conversation to Composition: The Role of Instruction in a Developmental Process." *Advances in Instructional Psychology.* Vol. 2. Ed. Robert Glaser. Hillsdale, NJ: Erlbaum, 1982.

Berger, Peter L., Brigette Berger, and Hansfried Kellner. *The Homeless Mind: Modernization and Consciousness.* New York: Random House, Vintage, 1974.

Berkenkotter, Carol. "Understanding a Writer's Awareness of Audience." *College Composition and Communication* 32 (1981): 388–99.

Berkow, Ira. "There's No Stopping Carter." *New York Times,* 23 Oct. 1986: B15.

Berlin, James. "Rhetoric and Ideology in the Writing Class" *College English* 50 (1988): 477–94.

Bernstein, Basil. *Class, Codes, and Control.* Vol. 1. *Theoretical Studies Toward a Sociology of Language.* London: Routledge & Kegan Paul, 1971.

Bissex, Glenda. *GYNS AT WRK: A Child Learns to Write and Read.* Cambridge: Harvard Univ. Press, 1980.

Bizzell, Patricia. "Cognition, Convention, and Certainty: What We Need to Know About Writing." *Pre/Text* 3 (Fall 1982): 213- 44.

———. "What Happens When Basic Writers Come to College?" *College Composition and Communication* 37 (1986): 294–301.

Bleich, David. *The Double Perspective: Language, Literacy, and Social Relations.* New York: Oxford Univ. Press, 1988.

Bohme, Gernot, and Nico Stehr, eds. *The Knowledge Society: The Growing Impact of Scientific Knowledge on Social Relations.* Boston: D. Reidel, 1986.

Brandt, Deborah. "Text and Context: How Writers Come to Mean." *Functional Approaches to Writing: Research Perspectives.* Ed. Barbara Couture. London: Frances Pinter, 1986. 93–107.

———. "Toward an Understanding of Context in Composition." *Written Communication* 3 (1986): 139–57.

———. "Writer, Context, and Text." Ph.D. diss., Indiana Univ. 1983.

Bridwell, Lillian. "Revising Strategies in Twelfth Grade Students' Transactional Writing." *Research in the Teaching of English* 14 (1980): 197–222.

Bruce, Bertram. "A Social Interaction Model of Reading." *Discourse Processes* 4 (1981): 273–311. ·

Carey, Susan. "The Child as Word Learner." *Linguistic Theory and Psychological Reality.* Ed. Morris Halles et al. Cambridge: The MIT Press, 1978. Quoted in Vande Kopple ("Some Exploratory Discourse").

Chafe, Wallace. "Integration and Involvement in Speaking, Writing, and Oral Literature." *Spoken and Written Language: Exploring Orality and Literacy.* Ed. Deborah Tannen. Norwood, NJ: Ablex, 1982. 33–54.

———. "Linguistic Differences Produced by Differences Between Speaking and Writing." *Literacy, Language, and Learning: The Nature and Consequences of Reading and Writing.* Ed. David R. Olson, Nancy Torrance, and Angela Hildyard. New York: Cambridge Univ. Press, 1985. 105–23.

———. "Writing in the Perspective of Speaking." *Studying Writing.* Eds. Charles R. Cooper and Sidney Greenbaum. Beverly Hills: Sage, 1986. 12–39.

Chafe, Wallace, and Jane Danielwicz. "Properties of Spoken and Written Language." *Comprehending Oral and Written Language.* Ed. Rosalyn Horowitz and S. Jay Samuels. Orlando: Academic Press, 1988.

Cochran-Smith, Marilyn. *The Making of a Reader.* Norwood, NJ: Ablex, 1984.

Cole, Michael, and Peg Griffin. "A Sociohistorical Approach to Remediation." *Literacy, Society, and Schooling: A Reader.* Eds. Suzanne de Castell, Allan Luke, and Kieran Egan. New York: Cambridge Univ. Press, 1986. 110–31.

Collins, James, and Sarah Michaels. "Speaking and Writing: Discourse Strategies and the Acquisition of Literacy." *The Social Construction of Literacy.* Ed. Jenny Cook-Gumperz. Cambridge: Cambridge Univ. Press, 1986. 207–22.

Comley, Nancy R., David Hamilton, Carl H. Klaus, Robert Scholes, and Nancy Sommers. *Fields of Writing: Readings Across the Disciplines.* New York: St. Martin's, 1984.

Cook-Gumperz, Jenny. "Literacy and Schooling: An Unchanging Equation?" *The Social Construction of Literacy.* Ed. Jenny Cook-Gumperz. New York: Cambridge Univ. Press, 1986. 16–44.

Cooper, Marilyn, and Michael Holzman. "More Talk About Protocols." *College Composition and Communication* 36 (1985): 97–100.

———. "Talking About Protocols." *College Composition and Communication* 34 (1983): 284–94.

Cressy, David. *Literacy and the Social Order: Reading and Writing in Tudor and Stuart England.* Cambridge: Cambridge Univ. Press, 1980.

Crismore, Avon. *Talking to Readers: Metadiscourse as Rhetorical Act.* New York: Peter Lang, 1989.

Culler, Jonathan. *Structural Poetics: Structuralism, Linguistics, and the Study of Literature.* Ithaca: Cornell Univ. Press, 1975.

Cummins, Jim. "Empowering Minority Students: A Framework for Intervention. *Harvard Educational Review* 56 (1986): 18–36.

D'Angelo, Frank. "Literacy and Cognition: A Developmental Perspective." *Literacy for Life: The Demand for Reading and Writing.* Eds. Richard W. Bailey and Robin Melanie Fosheim. New York: Modern Language Association, 1983. 97–114.

———. "Luria on Literacy: The Cognitive Consequences of Reading and Writing. *Literacy as a Human Problem.* Ed. James C. Raymond. University: Univ.of Alabama Press, 1982. 154–69.

———. "Paradigms as Structural Counterparts of *Topoi.*" *Linguistics, Stylistics, and the Teaching of Composition.* Ed. Donald McQuade. Akron: L & S Books, 1979.

Deely, John. *Introducing Semiotic: Its History and Doctrine.* Bloomington: Indiana Univ. Press, 1982.

Delpit, Lisa D. "Skills and Other Dilemmas of a Progressive Black Educator." *Harvard Educational Review* 56 (1986): 379–85.

Derrida, Jacques. *Of Grammatology.* Baltimore and London: The Johns Hopkins Univ. Press, 1974.

Dijk, Teun A. van. *Text and Context: Explorations in the Semantics and Pragmatics of Discourse.* London: Longman, 1977.

Dijk, Teun A. van, and Walter Kintsch. *Strategies of Discourse Comprehension.* New York: Academic Press, 1983.

Dobrin, David. "Protocols Once More." *College English* 48 (1986): 713–25.

Dyson, Anne Haas. "Emerging Alphabetic Literacy in School Contexts: Toward Defining the Gap Between School Curriculum and Child Mind." *Written Communication* 1 (1984): 5–55.

———. "Learning to Write/Learning to Do School: Emergent Writers' Interpretations of School Literacy Tasks." *Research in the Teaching of English* 18 (1984): 233–64.

Eco, Umberto. *The Role of the Reader: Explorations in the Semiotics of Texts.* Bloomington: Indiana Univ. Press, 1984.

Ede, Lisa, and Andrea Lunsford. "Audience Addressed/Audience Invoked: The Role of Audience in Composition Theory and Pedagogy." *College Composition and Communication* 35 (1984): 155–71.

Edwards, Derek, and Neil Mercer. *Common Knowledge: The Developments of Understanding in the Classroom.* London and New York: Metheun, 1987.

Egan, Kieran. "Individual Development in Literacy." *Literacy, Society, and Schooling*. Eds. Suzanne de Castell, Allan Luke, and Kieran Egan. New York: Cambridge Univ. Press, 1986. 243–55.

Eiseley, Loren. *The Invisible Pyramid*. New York: Charles Scribner's Sons, 1970.

Eisenstein, Deborah. *The Printing Press as an Agent of Change*. New York: Cambridge Univ. Press, 1979.

Emig, Janet. *The Composing Processes of Twelfth Graders*. NCTE Research Report No. 13. Urbana: National Council of Teachers of English, 1971.

———. "Writing as a Mode of Learning." *College Composition and Communication* 28 (1971): 122–28.

Faigley, Lester, Roger D. Cherry, David A. Jolliffe, and Anna M. Skinner. *Assessing Writers' Knowledge and Processes of Composing*. Norwood, NJ: Ablex, 1985.

Fein, Esther B. "Impresario Is Back in Moscow, For Now." *New York Times*, 11 May 1988, natl. ed.: 1

Ferreiro, Emilia, and Ana Teberosky. *Literacy Before Schooling*. Trans. Karen Goodman Castro. Exeter, NH: Heinemann Educational Books, 1983.

Fisher, Dennis F., and Charles W. Peters, eds. *Comprehension and the Competent Reader*. New York: Praeger, 1981.

Flower, Linda. "Entering Academic Discourse: The Power of Novice Strategies." Paper presented at the 1987 Conference on College Composition and Communication, Atlanta, Georgia.

———. "The Role of Task Representation in Reading to Write." Center for the Study of Writing Technical Report No. 6. Berkeley: Center for the Study of Writing, 1988.

———. "Writer-Based Prose: A Cognitive Basis for Problems in Writing." *College English* 41 (1979): 19–37.

Flower, Linda, and John R. Hayes. "The Cognition of Discovery: Defining a Rhetorical Problem." *College Composition and Communication* 31 (1980): 21–32.

———. "A Cognitive Process Theory of Writing." *College Composition and Communication* 32 (1981): 365–87.

———. "The Dynamics of Composing: Making Plans and Juggling Constraints." *Cognitive Processes in Writing: An Interdisciplinary Approach*. Eds. Lee W. Gregg and Erwin R. Steinberg. Hillsdale, NJ: Erlbaum, 1981.

———. "Images, Plans, and Prose: The Representation of Meaning in Writing. *Written Communication* 1 (1984): 120–60.

———. "The Pregnant Pause: An Inquiry into the Nature of Planning." *Research in the Teaching of English* 15 (1981): 229–44.

———. "Response to Marilyn Cooper and Michael Holzman, 'Talking About Protocols.'" *College Composition and Communication* 36 (1985): 94–99.

Franz, M.-L. von. "The Process of Individuation." *Man and His Symbols.* Ed. Carl Jung. New York: Dell, 1964.

Frawley, William. *Text and Epistemology: Advances in Discourse Processes.* Vol. 24. Norwood, NJ: Ablex, 1987.

Freedman, Sarah Warshauer, Anne Haas Dyson, Linda Flower, and Wallace Chafe. *Research in Writing: Past, Present, and Future.* Technical Report No. 1. Center for the Study of Writing. Berkeley: Univ. of California, 1987.

Freire, Paulo. *Pedagogy of the Oppressed.* New York: Seabury Press, 1973.

Freire, Paulo, and Donaldo Macedo. *Literacy: Reading the Word and the World.* South Hadley, MA: Bergin and Garvey, 1987.

Fulwiler, Toby. "How Well Does Writing Across the Curriculum Work?" *College English* 46 (1984): 113–25.

Fulwiler, Toby, and Art Young, eds. *Language Connections: Writing and Reading Across the Curriculum.* Urbana: National Council of Teachers of English, 1982.

Garfinkel, Harold. *Studies in Ethnomethodology.* New York: Prentice-Hall, 1967.

Gibson, Walker. *Persona: A Style Study for Readers and Writers.* New York: Random House, 1969.

Goldblatt, Eli. "Authority and Social Context: A Report on an Inner City High School Writing Project." Paper presented at the 1989 Conference on College Composition and Communication, Seattle.

Goodman, Yetta. "Children Coming to Know Literacy." *Emergent Literacy.* Eds. William H. Teale and Elizabeth Sulzby. Norwood, NJ: Ablex, 1986.

Goody, Jack. *The Interface Between the Written and the Oral.* Cambridge: Cambridge Univ. Press, 1987.

———. "Introduction." *Literacy in Traditional Societies.* Ed. Jack Goody. Cambridge: Cambridge Univ. Press, 1968. 1–27.

———. *The Logic of Writing and the Organization of Society.* Cambridge: Cambridge Univ. Press, 1986.

———. "Restricted Literacy in Northern Ghana." *Literacy in Traditional Societies.* Ed. Jack Goody. Cambridge: Cambridge Univ. Press, 1968.

Goody, Jack, and Ian Watt. "The Consequences of Literacy." *Literacy in*

Traditional Societies. Ed. Jack Goody. Cambridge: Cambridge Univ. Press, 1968. 27–68.

Gordon, Michael R. "Schultz to Press Soviets on Arm Pact." *New York Times,* 11 May 1988, natl. ed.: 4

Gough, Kathleen. "Implications of Literacy in Traditional China and India." *Literacy in Traditional Societies.* Ed. Jack Goody. Cambridge: Cambridge Univ. Press, 1968.

Gould, Christopher, and Kathleen Gould. "College Anthologies of Readings and Assumptions About Literacy." *College Composition and Communication* 37 (1986): 204–11.

Gould, Stephen J. "What Happens to Bodies if Genes Act for Themselves?" *Hen's Teeth and Horse's Toes.* New York: Norton, 1983.

Graff, Harvey J. *The Legacies of Literacy: Continuities and Contradictions in Western Society and Culture.* Bloomington: Indiana Univ. Press, 1986.

———. *The Literacy Myth: Literacy and Social Structure in the Nineteenth Century City.* New York: Academic Press, 1979.

Grant-Davie, Keith. "Rereading in the Writing Process." *Reader* (Spring 1989): 2–21.

Graves, Donald. *Writing: Teachers and Children at Work.* Exeter, NH: Heinemann Educational Books, 1982.

Greenfield, Patricia M. "Oral or Written Language: The Consequences for Cognitive Development in Africa, the United States, and England." *Language and Society* 15 (1972): 169–78.

Griffin, C. W. "Programs for Writing Across the Curriculum: A Report." *College Composition and Communication* 36 (1985): 398–403.

Gundlach, Robert, Joan B. McLane, Frances M. Stott, and Gillian Dowley McNamee. "Social Foundations of Children's Writing Development." *Children's Early Writing Development.* Ed. Marcia Farr. Norwood, NJ: Ablex, 1985.

Haas, Christina, and Linda Flower. "Rhetorical Reading Strategies and the Construction of Meaning." *College Composition and Communication* 39 (1988): 167–83.

Hairston, Maxine. "The Winds of Change: Thomas Kuhn and the Revolution in the Teaching of Writing." *College Composition and Communication* 33 (1982): 76–88.

Halliday, M. A. K. *Explorations in the Functions of Language.* London: Edward Arnold, 1973.

———. *Language as Social Semiotic: The Social Interpretation of Language and Meaning.* London: Edward Arnold, 1978.

———. *Learning How to Mean: Explorations in the Development of Language and Meaning.* London: Edward Arnold, 1975.

———. "Notes on Transitivity and Theme, Part 2." *Journal of Linguistics* 3 (1967): 199–244.

Halliday, M. A. K., and Ruqaiya Hasan. *Cohesion in English.* London: Longman, 1976.

Hamilton, David. "Interdisciplinary Writing." *College English* 41 (1980): 790–96.

Harste, Jerome C., Carolyn L. Burke, and Virginia Woodward. "Children's Language and World: Initial Encounters With Print." *Reader Meets Author/Bridging the Gap: A Psycholinguistic and Sociolinguistic Perspective.* Eds. Judith A. Langer and M. Trika Smith-Burke. Newark: International Reading Association, 1982.

Havelock, Eric. *The Literate Revolution in Greece and Its Cultural Consequences.* Princeton: Princeton Univ. Press, 1982.

———. *The Muse Learns to Write: Reflections on Orality and Literacy from Antiquity to the Present.* New Haven: Yale Univ. Press, 1980.

Hayes, John R., and Linda S. Flower. "Identifying the Organization of the Writing Process." *Cognitive Processes in Writing.* Eds. Lee W. Gregg and Erwin R. Steinberg. Hillsdale, NJ: Erlbaum, 1980.

Heath, Shirley Brice. "Critical Factors in Literacy Development." *Literacy, Society, and Schooling: A Reader.* Eds. Suzanne de Castell, Allan Luke, and Kieran Egan. New York: Cambridge Univ. Press, 1986. 209–29.

———. *Ways with Words: Language, Life, and Work in Communities and Classrooms.* New York: Cambridge Univ. Press, 1984.

Heath, Shirley Brice, with Charlene Thomas. "The Achievement of Preschool Literacy for Mother and Child." *Awakening to Literacy.* Eds. Hillel Goelman, Antoinette Oberg, and Frank Smith. Exeter, NH: Heinemann Educational Books, 1984. 51–72.

Herrington, Anne J. "Classrooms as Forums for Reasoning and Writing." *College Composition and Communication* 36 (1985): 404–13.

Hirsch, E. D., Jr. "Comments on *Profession 88.*" *Profession 88.* New York: Modern Language Association, 1988.

———. *Cultural Literacy.* Boston: Houghton Mifflin, 1987.

Horner, Vivian. "A Psycholinguist's Response." *Black Dialects and Reading.* Ed. Bernice E. Cullinan. Urbana: National Council of Teachers of English, 1974.

Hunt, Russell. "A Horse Named Hans, a Boy Named Shawn: The Herr Von Osten Theory of Response to Writing." *Writing and Response:*

Theory, Practice, and Research. Ed. Chris M. Anson. Urbana: National Council of Teachers of English, 1989. 80–100.

Iser, Wolfgang. *The Act of Reading: A Theory of Aesthetic Response.* Baltimore: The Johns Hopkins Univ. Press, 1978.

———. "Texts and Readers." *Discourse Processes* 3 (1980): 327–43.

Kintgen, Eugene. *The Perception of Poetry.* Bloomington: Indiana Univ. Press, 1983.

Kirsch, Irwin S., and Ann Jungeblut. *Literacy: Profiles of America's Young Adults.* Princeton: Educational Testing Service, n.d.

Kjolseth, Rolf. "Making Sense: Natural Language and Shared Knowledge in Understanding." *Advances in the Sociology of Language.* Vol. 1. Ed. Joshua A. Fishman. The Hague: Mouton, 1971.

Knoblauch, C. H., and Lil Brannon. "Writing as Learning Through the Curriculum." *College English* 45 (1983): 465–74.

Kozol, Jonathan. *Illiterate America.* New York: Doubleday, Anchor, 1985.

Leichter, Hope Jensen. "Families as Environments for Literacy." *Awakening to Literacy.* Eds. Hillel Goelman, Antoinette Oberg, and Frank Smith. Exeter, NH: Heinemann Educational Books, 1984. 38–50.

Lockeridge, Kenneth. *Literacy in Colonial New England: An Enquiry Into the Social Context of Literacy in the Early Modern West.* New York: Norton, 1974.

Luria, Alexander. *Cognitive Development: Its Cultural and Social Foundations.* Trans. Martin Lopez-Morillas and Lyn Solotaroff. Ed. Michael Cole. Cambridge: Cambridge Univ. Press, 1976.

———. *Language and Cognition.* Ed. James V. Wertsch. New York: Wiley, 1981.

McDermott, R. P. "Social Relations as Contexts for Learning in School." *Harvard Educational Review* 47 (1977): 198–213.

McGee, Lea M. "Good and Poor Readers' Ability to Distinguish Among and Recall Ideas on Different Levels of Importance." *Directions in Reading: Research and Instruction. Thirtieth Yearbook of the National Reading Conference.* Ed. Michael L. Kamil. Washington, DC: National Reading Conference, 1981.

MacGinitie, Walter H., and Ruth K. MacGinitie. "Teaching Students Not to Read." *Literacy, Society, and Schooling: A Reader.* Eds. Suzanne de Castell, Allan Luke, and Kieran Egan. New York: Cambridge Univ. Press, 1986. 256–69.

Maimon, Elaine. "Maps and Genres: Exploring Connections in the Arts and Sciences." *Composition and Literature: Bridging the Gap.* Ed. Winifred Horner. Chicago: Univ. of Chicago Press, 1983. 110–25.

Maimon, Elaine, Gerald L. Belcher, Gail W. Hearn, Barbara F. Nodine, and Finbarr W. O'Connor. *Writing in the Arts and Sciences.* Cambridge, MA: Winthrop, 1981.

Malinowski, Bronislaw. *Coral Gardens and Their Magic: A Study of the Methods of Tilling the Soil and of Agricultural Rites in the Trobriand Islands.* Vol 2. New York: American Book Co., 1935.

————. "The Problem of Meaning in Primitive Languages." *The Meaning of Meaning: A Study of the Influence of Language Upon Thought and of the Science of Symbolism.* Eds. C. K. Ogden and I. A. Richards. New York: Harcourt, Brace, 1923.

Mallioux, Steven. *Interpretive Conventions: The Reader in the Study of American Fiction.* Ithaca: Cornell Univ. Press, 1982.

Moffett, James. "Writing, Inner Speech, and Meditation." *College English* 44 (1982): 231–46.

Murray, Donald. "Writing as Process: How Writing Finds Its Own Meaning." *Eight Approaches to Teaching Composition.* Eds. Timothy R. Donovan and Ben W. McClelland. Urbana: National Council of Teachers of English, 1980. 3–20.

Newman, J. M., ed. *Whole Language: Theory and Practice.* Exeter, NH: Heinemann Educational Books, 1985.

Nystrand, Martin. *The Structure of Written Communication.* Orlando: Academic Press, 1986.

Olson, David R. "The Language of Instruction: The Literate Bias of Schooling. *Schooling and the Acquisition of Knowledge.* Eds. Richard Anderson, Rand Spiro, and William E. Montague. Hillsdale, NJ: Erlbaum 1977. 65–89.

————. "'See! Jumping!' Some Oral Antecedents of Literacy." *Awakening to Literacy.* Eds. Hillel Goelman, Antoinette A. Oberg, and Frank Smith. Exeter, NH: Heinemann Educational Books, 1984.

————. "Some Social Aspects of Meaning in Oral and Written Language." *Social Foundations of Language and Thought.* Ed. David R. Olson. New York: Norton, 1980. 90–110.

————. "From Utterance to Text: The Bias of Language in Speech and Writing. *Harvard Educational Review* 47 (1977): 257–81.

————. "Writing: The Divorce of the Author from the Text." *Exploring Speaking-Writing Relationships: Connections and Contrasts.* Eds. Barry M. Kroll and Roberta J. Vann. Urbana: National Council of Teachers of English, 1981. 99–110.

Olson, David R., and Angela Hildyard. "Writing and Literal Meaning." *The*

Psychology of Written Language: Developmental and Educational Perspectives. Ed. Margaret Martlew. New York: Wiley, 1983.

Ong, Walter J. *Orality and Literacy: The Technologizing of the Word.* New York: Methuen, 1982.

———. "Reading, Technology, and Human Consciousness." *Literacy as a Human Problem.* Ed. James C. Raymond. University: Univ. of Alabama Press, 1982. 170–201.

———. "The Writer's Audience Is Always a Fiction." *PMLA* 90 (1975): 9–21.

———. "Writing Is a Technology That Restructures Thought." *The Written Word: Literacy in Transition.* Ed. Gerd Baumann. Oxford: Clarendon Press, 1986.

Paris, Scott G., and Myer Myers. "Comprehension Monitoring in Good and Poor Readers." *Journal of Reading Behavior* 13 (1981): 5–22.

Park, Douglas. "The Meanings of Audience." *College English* 44 (1982): 247–57.

Pattison, Robert. *On Literacy: The Politics of the Word From Homer to the Age of Rock.* New York: Oxford Univ. Press, 1982.

Perelman, Les. "The Context of Classroom Writing." *College English* 48 (1986): 471–78.

Perkins, David A. *A History of Modern Poetry From the 1890s to the High Modernist Mode.* Cambridge: Harvard Univ. Press, Belknap Press, 1976.

Perl, Sondra. "The Composing Processes of Unskilled College Writers." *Research in the Teaching of English* 13 (1979): 317–36.

Piaget, Jean. *The Language and Thought of the Child.* Trans. Marjorie Gabin. New York: Harcourt, Brace, 1932.

Pianko, Sharon. "A Description of the Composition Processes of College Freshmen Writers." *Research in the Teaching of English* 13 (1979): 5–22.

Popper, Karl R. *Objective Knowledge: An Evolutionary Approach.* London: Oxford Univ. Press, 1972.

Prince, Ellen. "Toward a Taxonomy of Given-New Information." *Radical Pragmatics.* Ed. Peter Cole. New York: Academic Press, 1981. 223–55.

Prince, Gerald. *Narratology.* New York: Mouton, 1982.

Pritchard, Ruie Jane. "Effects on Student Writing of Teacher Training in the National Writing Project Model." *Written Communication* 9 (1987): 51–67.

Profession 88. New York: Modern Language Association, 1988.

Ricoeur, Paul. *Interpretation Theory: Discourse and the Surplus of Meaning.* Fort Worth: Texas Christian Univ. Press, 1976.

Riesman, David. "The Oral and Written Tradition." *Explorations in Communication.* Eds. Edmund Carpenter and Marshall McLuhan. Boston: Beacon, 1960. 109–16.

Rohman, D. Gordon. "Pre-writing: The Stage of Discovery in the Writing Process." *College Composition and Communication* 16 (1965): 106–12.

Rommetveit, Ragnar. *On Message Structure: A Framework for the Study of Language and Communication.* New York: Wiley, 1974.

Rose, Mike. "Narrowing the Mind and Page: Remedial Writers and Cognitive Reductionism." *College Composition and Communication* 39 (1988): 267–302.

———. "Rigid Rules, Inflexible Plans, and the Stifling of Language: A Cognitivist Analysis of Writer's Block." *College Composition and Communication* 31 (1980): 389–401.

Rosenblatt, Louise. *The Reader, The Text, The Poem: The Transactional Theory of the Literary Work.* Carbondale: Southern Illinois Univ. Press, 1978.

Roth, Robert G. "The Evolving Audience: Alternatives to Audience Accommodation." *College Composition and Communication* 33 (1987): 47–55.

Rubin, Andee. "A Theoretical Taxonomy of the Differences Between Oral and Written Language." *Theoretical Issues in Reading Comprehension: Perspectives from Cognitive Psychology, Linguistics, Artificial Intelligence, and Education.* Eds. Rand J. Spiro, Bertram C. Bruce, and William F. Brewer. Hillsdale, NJ: Erlbaum, 1980. 411–38.

Rubin, Donald L. "Introduction: Four Dimensions of Social Construction in Written Communication." *The Social Construction of Written Communication.* Eds. Bennett A. Rafoth and Donald L. Rubin. Norwood, NJ: Ablex, 1988. 1–33.

———. "Social Cognition and Written Communication." *Written Communication* 1 (1984): 211–45.

Schieffelin, Bambi B., and Marilyn Cochran-Smith. "Learning to Read Culturally: Literacy Before Schooling." *Awakening to Literacy.* Eds. Hillel Goelman, Antoinette Oberg, and Frank Smith. Exeter, NH: Heinemann Educational Books, 1984. 3–23.

Scholes, Robert. "Replies to E. D. Hirsch, Jr." *Profession 88.* New York: Modern Language Association, 1988.

———. "Three Views of Education: Nostalgia, History, and Voodoo" (a review-essay). *College English* 50 (1988): 323–32.

Scinto, Leonard. *Written Language and Psychological Development.* New York: Academic Press, 1986.

Scribner, Sylvia, and Michael Cole. *The Psychology of Literacy.* Cambridge: Harvard Univ. Press, 1981.

Shanklin, Nancy. "Relating Reading and Writing: Developing a Transactional Theory of the Writing Process." Ph.D. diss., Indiana Univ., 1980.

Skinner, B. F. *Beyond Freedom and Dignity.* New York: Knopf, 1972.

Smith, Frank. "Demonstrations, Engagement, and Sensitivity." *Essays Into Literacy.* Exeter, NH: Heinemann Educational Books, 1983. 95–106.

Snow, Catherine. "Literacy and Language: Relationships During the Preschool Years." *Harvard Educational Review* 53 (1983): 165–89.

Soltow, Lee, and Edward Stevens. *The Rise of Literacy and the Common School in the United States: A Socioeconomic Analysis to 1870.* Chicago: Univ. of Chicago Press, 1981.

Steiner, George. "Dying Is an Art." *Language and Silence: Essays on Language, Literature, and the Inhuman.* New York: Atheneum, 1970. 295–302.

Street, Brian. *Literacy in Theory and Practice.* Cambridge: Cambridge Univ. Press, 1984.

Sturgeon, Theodore. "It." *Famous Monster Tales.* Collected by Basil Davenport. Princeton: D. Van Nostrand, 1967.

Suleiman, Susan R., and Inge Crosman, eds. *The Reader in the Text: Essays in Audience and Interpretation.* Princeton: Princeton Univ. Press, 1980.

Tannen, Deborah. *Conversational Style: Analyzing Talk Among Friends.* Norwood, NJ: Ablex, 1984.

———. "The Oral-Literate Continuum in Discourse." *Spoken and Written Language: Exploring Orality and Literacy.* Ed. Deborah Tannen. Norwood, NJ: Ablex, 1982. 33–54.

———. "Relative Focus on Involvement in Oral and Written Discourse." *Literacy, Language, and Learning: The Nature and Consequences of Reading and Writing.* Eds. David R. Olson, Nancy Torrance, and Angela Hildyard. New York: Cambridge Univ. Press, 1985. 124–47.

Taylor, Denny. *Family Literacy: Young Children Learning to Read and Write.* Exeter, NH: Heinemann Educational Books, 1983.

Teale, William H. "Reading to Young Children: Its Significance for Literacy Development." *Awakening to Literacy.* Eds. Hillel Goelman, Antoi-

nette Oberg, and Frank Smith. Exeter, NH: Heinemann Educational
Books, 1984. 110–21.

———. "Toward a Theory of How Children Learn to Read and Write
Naturally." *Composing and Comprehending.* Ed. Julie M. Jensen. Urbana: ERIC Clearinghouse on Reading and Communication Skills,
1984. 127–42.

Teale, William H., and Elizabeth Sulzby, eds. *Emergent Literacy.* Norwood, NJ: Ablex, 1986.

Torrance, Nancy, and David R. Olson. "Oral and Literate Competencies
in the Early School Years." *Literacy, Language, and Learning: The
Nature and Consequences of Reading and Writing.* Eds. David R.
Olson, Nancy Torrance, and Angela Hildyard. New York: Cambridge
Univ. Press, 1985. 256–84.

Tuman, Myron. *A Preface to Literacy: An Inquiry Into Pedagogy, Practice,
and Progress.* University: Univ. of Alabama Press, 1987.

Vande Kopple, William J. "Given and New Information and Some Aspects
of the Structures, Semantics, and Pragmatics of Written Texts." *Studying Writing.* Eds. Charles Cooper and Sidney Greenbaum. Beverly
Hills: Sage, 1986. 72–111.

———. "Some Exploratory Discourse on Metadiscourse." *College Composition and Communication* 36 (1985): 82–93.

Vipond, Douglas, and Russell Hunt. "Point Driven Understanding: Pragmatic and Cognitive Dimensions of Literary Reading." *Poetics* 13
(1984): 261–77.

———. "Shunting Information or Making Contact?: Assumptions for
Research on Aesthetic Reading." *English Quarterly* 20 (1987) 131–36.

Vygotsky, Lev. *Thought and Language.* Ed. and trans. Eugenia Hanfmann
and Gertrude Vakar. Cambridge: The MIT Press, 1962.

Walkerdine, Valerie. "From Context to Text: A Psychosemiotic Approach
to Abstract Thought." *Children Thinking Through Language.* Ed. Michael Beveridge. London: Edward Arnold, 1982. 129–55.

Walters, Keith. "Language, Logic, and Literacy." Paper presented at the
Modern Language Association "Right to Literacy" Conference, Colum-
bus, Ohio, Sept. 1988.

Welch, Kathleen. "Ideology and Freshman Textbook Production: The
Role of Theory in Writing Pedagogy." *College Composition and Communication* 38 (1987): 269–82.

Wells, Gordon. *The Meaning Makers: Children Learning Language and
Using Language to Learn.* Portsmouth, NH: Heinemann Educational
Books, 1986.

White, James Boyd. "The Invisible Discourse of the Law: Reflections on Legal Literacy and General Education." *Literacy for Life: The Demands for Reading and Writing.* Eds. Richard W. Bailey and Robin Melanie Fosheim. New York: Modern Language Association, 1983. 139–50.

Williams, Raymond. *Communications.* Rev. ed. London: Chatto and Windus, 1960.

Wilson, John. "The Properties, Purposes, and Promotion of Literacy." *Literacy, Society, and Schooling.* Eds. Suzanne de Castell, Allan Luke, and Kieran Egan. New York: Cambridge Univ. Press, 1986. 27–36.

Winograd, Peter N. "Strategic Difficulties in Summarizing Texts." *Reading Research Quarterly* 19 (1983–84): 404–25.

Witte, Stephen P. "Topical Structure and Revision: An Exploratory Study." *College Composition and Communication* 34 (1983): 313–41.

Index

Abstraction. *See* "Strong-text" literacy; Writing; Written language
Akinasso, F. Niyi, 129n. 1
Alphabet, 23, 25, 61, 99, 125
Anderson, Alonzo B., 112
Anonymity. *See* "Strong-text" literacy; Writing; Written language
Applebee, Arthur, 134n. 5
Atwell, Margaret, 50
Atwell, Nancie, 121, 122
Audience, 5, 48, 49, 69–73
Audience awareness, 59, 69, 71, 86
Augustine, Dorothy, 69
Autonomy. *See* "Strong-text" literacy; Written language

Bar-Hillel, Yehosua, 73
Bartholomae, David, 135n. 15
Bates, Elizabeth, 112
Bay Area Writing Project, 121
Bazerman, Charles, 119, 135n. 15
Bereiter, Carl, 136n. 18
Berkenkotter, Carol, 70
Berlin, James, 122, 136n. 19
Bernstein, Basil, 106–7, 134n. 5
Bissex, Glenda, 134n. 8
Bizzell, Patricia, 33, 119, 120
Bleich, David, 103
Brandt, Deborah, 131nn. 8, 11
Brannon, Lil, 135n. 15
Bridwell, Lillian, 50
Bruce, Bertram, 132n. 4
Burke, Carolyn, 133n. 3, 134n. 8

"Casual meaning." *See* Written language
Chafe, Wallace, 129n. 1

Cherry, Roger, 70
Cochran-Smith, Marilyn, 112, 134n. 7
Cohesion, 9, 61, 76–79
Cole, Michael, 7, 25, 26, 103, 115
Collins, James, 106, 129n. 1
Collocation, 65
Comley, Nancy R., 136n. 15
Communicative dynamism, 62–64
Composing process: cognition in, 50; differences between expert and novice, Table 1, 52; evolving text in, 50, 51, 54–55; of expert writer, 52–56; and intersubjectivity, 49–50, 56; of novice, 52–55; pedagogy in, 33; pragmatic meaning in, 37; reading and planning by expert and novice, Table 2, 54; scanning in, 54. *See also* Metacommunication; Reading and writing
Composition studies, 1; cognitive perspectives in, 11; process movement in, 33–35; social/antisocial tension in, 1–2, 10–11; status of text in, 11
Context, 4, 6–7, 9, 30, 34; and composing, 35, 38–39, 45, 49–50; definitions of, 29–30; and intersubjectivity, 49, 122; and literacy, 3, 103, 105; of pragmatic action, 4, 6, 38, 57, 125; in reading and writing, 42–43, 51, 57–58; and reference, 113; semantic, 38, 91; of situation, 124; social, 112, 126; in speaking, 6, 28; in strong-text accounts, 31; and text, 5, 33, 45, 50, 54–55, 78, 119; transcendence of, 8, 32; "working," 5, 31, 38–39, 45, 48. *See also* Decontextualization; Literacy; Reading and writing

153

Deborah Brandt is Director of Intermediate Composition at the University of Wisconsin–Madison. A recipient of the NCTE Promising Researcher Award in 1984, she is a member of the National Council on Research in English. Her articles have appeared in *College English* and *Written Communication*.